There's a Book in Every Expert (that's you!)

How to write your
credibility-building book
in six months

Jennifer Jones

Copyright © 2020 by Jennifer Diann Jones.
All rights reserved.

This book or any portion thereof may not be reproduced or used in any manner whatsoever without the express written permission of the publisher except for the use of brief quotations in a book review.

Strenuous attempts have been made to credit all copyrighted materials used in this book. All such materials and trademarks, which are referenced in this book, are the full property of their respective copyright owners. Every effort has been made to obtain copyright permission for material quoted in this book. Any omissions will be rectified in future editions.

Printed in the United Kingdom
First Printing, 2020

ISBN: 978-1-8380011-0-0 (Paperback)
ISBN: 978-1-8380011-1-7 (eBook)

Maggie Cat Books
Portsmouth, Hants
PO3 6NJ

jennifer@ewc.coach

CONTENTS

FOREWORD 5

CHAPTER 1: Who is this book for?...13

CHAPTER 2: But I'm not an author..15

CHAPTER 3: How will writing a book help my business? 21

CHAPTER 4: Why should you listen to me about writing?........ 25

CHAPTER 5: What help might you need? 27

CHAPTER 6: Getting started 33

CHAPTER 7: Write little and often
– Especially when you don't want to..................... 39

CHAPTER 8: First drafts... 51

CHAPTER 9: Writer's block, impostor syndrome, and
other things that keep writers up at night............. 59

CHAPTER 10: Clearing your head.. 71

CHAPTER 11: The importance of boundaries.............................. 73

CHAPTER 12: Managing long writing sessions 77

CHAPTER 13: Finding your voice 79

CHAPTER 14: Keeping up the momentum 83

CHAPTER 15: First revision 89

CHAPTER 16: Second revision 97

CHAPTER 17: Beta readers 105

CHAPTER 18: What happens when you work with an editor?.. 111

CHAPTER 19: Dealing with criticism 115

CHAPTER 20: Dealing with praise 121

CHAPTER 21: Respecting intellectual property 127

CHAPTER 22: Practise safe writing 135

CHAPTER 23: Staying organised 141

CHAPTER 24: Recommended reading 145

WORKS CITED 151

AFTERWORD 155

FOREWORD

"LAURYN, I loved your book Grow Your Tribe and I'd be honoured if you'd write the foreword for my own forthcoming book", asked Jennifer during our wonderful meeting at a business conference for entrepreneurial women in May 2019.

As a published author myself, you would expect me to feel an overwhelming wave of excitement, as it's generally recognised as an honour to be asked to write the foreword for another author's work. To be asked is a silent nod that you have 'made it' and you have the credibility and authority to introduce a fellow author's creation to an expectant and waiting world.

Alas, not for me.

That small nagging voice of impostor syndrome mocked me as I said "yes, I'd be honoured to". This is my first foreword, and this is my first formal recognition of having 'made it' as an author. I am exhilarated and terrified in equal measure.

Imposter syndrome is a strange feeling. Speaking from experience as an author, I know there will always be a deadline looming ahead. The blissful lull of procrastination, knowing I have months to finish my work, and yet, life strangely moves as if on fast forward. The deadline looms ever closer.

I wait in a dreamlike pause in anticipation of receiving the first draft of Jennifer's new book, but also life continues in that same blissful denial. Surely, I haven't really been asked to write a foreword for this incredible book. I must've misheard. What do *I* know about writing?

If Jennifer only knew the raw agonies I faced when I wrote my first book Grow Your Tribe, then I was sure I would be found out and that coveted invitation to write this foreword would be promptly rescinded.

Where does this feeling come from? We women have faced challenges throughout history; the echoes of these remain ever present in our daily lives. It's hard to shrug off these experiences. In our careers, we have shown up in our work and not been surprised when those inevitable glass ceilings or raised eyebrows appear. Times are changing and this is a new world we are living in, but our scars from the past are lurking there.

We know the fear of shouting and sharing our expertise out into the world because of an ingrained inner belief that our 'stories' are not important. Who will listen to me? Our voice falters and we fall silent. We doubt that we *really* can write this, and we put our dreams of writing about our passions and our expertise to one side. "Maybe one day I will face my fears and write that book", we cry!

Now, I didn't feel powerless when considering authoring my first book, but I was afraid. I had no direction, no expert of my own to call upon. I was floundering in the dark, and I was not set up for success from the very beginning.

I made many mistakes, and I developed my writing skills the hard way. We all know that our mistakes help us to grow, but had I had the opportunity to follow in Jennifer's 'tried and tested' footsteps when I became a writer, I would have saved myself much angst, frustration and rework from floundering in the dark. Jennifer now removes that scenario like tearing a page from a book.

She appears as a bright beacon in that dark tunnel, lighting the way for women entrepreneurs to find and write about their own expertise. To find their courage and create their masterpiece with confidence and under the very clear direction she presents in her book.

On meeting her bright beacon of guidance in this book, our warriors within awaken. We open our copies of Jennifer's book to find and connect with what speaks directly to us. Her book presents us with exactly what we need.

Jennifer's book builds my confidence in my power as a woman entrepreneur and in why I should be confidently and passionately contributing to my field of expertise. I close her book with that reinforcement of why I am the *only* expert who can successfully bring *my* book to life. If there is anything to be afraid of in life, then it is not my expertise or my voice.

Jennifer assumes we have no prior knowledge, literary skill or need for perfection before reading her book. She wants our beauty to shine through all our inner fears and imperfections, to work with her to grow, to grant ourselves the permission for those words to freely flow whilst we create our masterpieces.

What do you think makes you an expert? As a woman entrepreneur, I am often asked by my peers how to break through the doubt of owning your expertise to write that book. I tell these incredible budding authors that if people are investing in your business, your products and your services then they are already invested in YOU. You are an expert by default. Own that expertise with pride and celebrate it.

In her book, Jennifer gently guides her readers in the belief that you don't need to 'know it all'; all you really need is the confidence in the knowledge and beliefs that you have when you sit at your keyboard to write.

My own journey to creating my first book was a daunting, exciting, chaotic and a very scattergun experience. I remember forming my seedling idea: the desire that I wanted to write a book about growing a tribe and successfully selling to them. The imposter syndrome wasted no time in jumping in.

- What do I write about?
- Do I have the expert knowledge to put myself 'out there'?
- Would my experiences in my area of expertise bring true transformation to others?
- How would I bring all of these story threads together?
- How will I navigate my writing journey without being 'found out' that I'm not an expert author?
- Who would buy my book?

I knew I was guaranteed at least three sales of my finished work. That's a copy for my mum, a copy for my sister and one for my good friend. "I'm on a winning streak already", I told myself.

I knew beyond a shadow of doubt that I had a great book within me. But where would I start? I sat looking at my computer screen. The cursor blinking. Nothing. I type 'the'. I hit backspace. I type 'hello'. I hit backspace. I type 'Welcome' and you guessed it: I hit backspace, leaned back and sighed, and after 3 hours I typed 'I give up.'

I wasted too many good writing hours unproductively figuring out how to get started. How to plan my book. How to write it. How to build successful writing habits and productive routines into my writing days. I was absolutely lost.

I'm not a natural born writer, so finding my flow was difficult. And there I was, a budding best-selling author with no flow, no defined writing style and no routine.

Jennifer's tips are invaluable, and I wish I had had a copy of her book on my desk when I started. She walks her readers through concepts such as how to write little and often, especially during those moments when everything in your body is shouting at you to stop and go and do something else. I did not want to sit down to write most days. I had no routine. A spark of enlightenment at the strangest of times would see me hurry to my laptop. Never mind that it was 3am! My journey as a writer has been bumpy, eventually with my arriving at the place of understanding the importance of having a defined writing routine to boost my creativity and productivity.

If only I had had Jennifer's book to guide me through this process - to guide me through the importance of finding my personal writing ritual. And whilst writing, then understanding those questions around how long should my book be? When do I stop writing? How do I know when I can type 'The END' with confidence?

Creating a book is like creating a piece of art. We are painting our words of wisdom on a canvas. And like any artist, the secret is knowing when to stop. Good writing is an art in itself. How will you finish your story?

I initially knew I had a great story to tell. I had a business story that I wanted to share. I wanted to bring my insights, my expertise and my tips to the audience who were going to be reading my book. But, the impostor within quickly jumped to the fore.

My first writing experience was just that. An experience. And not a good one at that! Six months later, after exiting the cloudy blur of solid writing, I had completed the first draft of my book. And looking back it feels easy to say, I completed my book in six months, but if I had had Jennifer's guidance by my side during my writing journey, then I am certain I would have completed my book in three!

The first round of beta reader feedback made it clear my first revision had reflected my jumbled and haphazard approach to my writing. The initial relief of finishing my first draft had vanished. It was just that, a draft. I was not finished. I had heavy revisions to make, and it was painful. I was learning alone and learning the hard way.

In this book, Jennifer quickly gets the reader to grips of dealing with writer's block, mastering the dreaded imposter syndrome, and other things that keep us budding writers up at night.

I now write my very first foreward after reading this book, my impostor syndrome receding into the shadows like a banished spectre which has no permission to return. I am now confident of banishing writer's block in future.

Jennifer takes us through how to correctly use humour and sarcasm so that we're not offending our readers, unless our point is to be controversial, and then we project that boldness with empowerment!

She asks us to ask this question: How do you want your readers to *feel* when they're reading your work?

And again, Jennifer shows you how to find your momentum, whilst you're writing. To find balance in harnessing those spurts of energy in tandem with walking away from the laptop to get other things done. It's so easy to write for hours and hours, and then conversely difficult when trying to find that same momentum in the midst of those dry spells when we sit watching a blank screen. The cursor flashing, no words pouring out. She helps you out of this feast or famine cycle.

Planning is everything. Set yourself up for success. And Jennifer's book takes you through the process of setting yourself up for success. Your creativity is in safe hands, as she shows you how to create your early structure and form your initial drafts.

Jennifer's support doesn't stop there. Her book continues to take you through the process of what happens once you put your pen down, and finish your first draft, your second draft or third.

She effortlessly guides you through the proofreading, editing and beta reading stages and most importantly, how to protect your finished work. I must mention, protect your writing from damage or deletion. I did not. If you're writing on paper, likewise, do not to let the family dog near your homework!

So, as Jennifer will soon go on to say, 'do not let the word expertise throw you. If you run a business, you are an expert.'

There is an audience out there of people eagerly waiting to hear from you. They will be excited to have a copy of your authored book in their hands. You are an expert, so unleash your knowledge, own your passion and allow your words to flow!

Lauryn Bradley

Author of *Grow Your Tribe - How to Scale + Skyrocket Your Business by Loving Your Audience*

CHAPTER 1
WHO IS THIS BOOK FOR?

THIS book is primarily for women who run service-based businesses who want to establish their authority by writing and publishing a book in their area of expertise. That is not to say, though, that it won't be useful for other nonfiction writers - it will be, but my examples are crafted with business women in mind.

Don't let the word *expertise* throw you. If you run a business, you're an expert. Are there people who know more about your field? Almost certainly. However, there are a lot more people who know less about your field and who need to know what you know. Your book need not be the final word on your subject.

Instead, think of your book as a way to join the conversation in your field. In this conversation, you're not trying to teach the other experts anything (though all experts know they still have much to learn); instead, you are sharing your perspective or approach. Also, remember that since you're joining a conversation, you're just trying to be heard - you're not trying to talk over everyone else; this is an important distinction, especially for women writers who are dealing with a lifetime of being told to let others speak first.

Your book is valuable to your potential clients because it is the perfect way for them to really get to know you and how you think about your services and business. Writing a book for your future clients is a brilliant way to market your business. As they read the book, they'll find out all they need to know about what you do. Also, for readers who don't become clients - your book will allow them to benefit from your thinking; by writing it, you're expanding your reach in the world.

Are you thinking, 'but if I tell them all of what I do in a book that they buy on Amazon for a few pounds, why would they hire me?' They'll hire you because your book will convince them that you really know your topic. Sure, you can explain how to do what you do or teach them something in a couple of hundred pages, but that will never be the same as working with you.

Some readers will read your book, apply what they can on their own, and then move on with their lives. These readers are not your ideal, paying audience. Your ideal, paying audience is looking to learn who you are, what you do, and crucially what you can do for them. The long form of a book gives you the opportunity to lay that out in an easy to navigate format.

In short: your book will help you build your tribe.

CHAPTER 2
BUT I'M NOT AN *AUTHOR*

MANY (if not most) people who have never written a book imagine that an 'author' spends all day, every day writing. During this writing time, these 'authors' pour perfectly polished prose onto the page. At the end of a few weeks or months, they have enough words to count as a book, and they send the manuscript off to the publishers who jump all over themselves to publish it as quickly as possible...

[cue screeching brake noise here]

This isn't how it works. Inexperienced writers often plan to spend hours every day being very serious about their writing. Some will *even* manage to actually do this for a day or two. However, life gets in the way.

When we try to write this way, we set ourselves up for failure. If we believe we 'must' do something a certain way (or not at all) and our reality doesn't match that imagined ideal, we tend to get frustrated and quit.

To help you avoid setting yourself up for disappointment, let's look at how writing actually works.

Full-time authors (those who earn the majority of their income through their writing) do often write for several hours a day. However, a great many authors have other commitments: they are parents, business owners, and/or employees (to name just a few of the plethora of commitments they might have). These authors find ways to make their writing fit around their lives.

On a good day, this will involve setting aside an hour or two to focus on writing. On an average day, they'll be able to find two or three 30-minute writing sessions spread over the course of the day. On a bad day, they'll find a way to spend 10 minutes with their writing project. On an exceptionally bad day, the writing gets shoved to the side while they deal with whatever crisis has occurred.

If you've done the maths, you may well be wondering if it's really possible to write a book in as little as 8 or 9 hours a week. If you're organised and focused during those few hours, then yes, it is possible.

You'll have noticed that our imaginary writers do at least a little writing every day, except the exceptionally bad days. Why would someone who has had a tough day at work bother spending just 10 minutes with the book they're writing? Because it's worth it.

Writers who at least check in with their projects each day, write more. They write more because the ideas stay fresh in their minds – our amazing brains keep working on problems long after we've taken our conscious attention away from them. They write more than those who write by fits and starts because they are familiar with their projects.

Familiarity, in this case, usually breeds comfort rather than contempt. Familiarity also keeps the project, and any problems they're having with it, from taking on monstrous proportions.

Think about that last point for a minute. How often have you found that the anxiety before an unpleasant or difficult event turned out to be worse than the event itself? Have you put off going to the dentist for fear of what might happen, only to finally go and simply have your teeth polished and checked? The same is true of a difficult writing project. The longer you avoid working on it, the scarier it will seem. However, once you finally screw up the courage to open the document and look at the problem you were trying to sort out, you'll find out that fixing it involves no more than moving a paragraph or rewriting a few sentences – it's an anti-climax compared to the apocalyptic disaster you had envisioned. We'll return to this idea of checking in on your book in Chapter 7, 'Write Little and Often'.

BUT PEOPLE LIKE ME CAN'T BE 'WRITERS'

If you've overcome the time-constraints objection, you may find your brain throwing up other objections; chief amongst these is often that 'people like me don't write'.

Most often, this means that the would-be author in question is convinced that working class people, women, women who haven't been to university (or who 'only' have BA degrees), or people who belong to some other group don't write books. My knee-jerk reaction to such objections is to say '*balderdash*'.

Since I know that's not a terribly useful reaction, I'll give a more considered one here.

'Society' has a great many expectations about what certain types of people can and cannot do. I have come up against these expectations myself – both of my parents worked for the US Postal Service; in other words, they were what Americans call 'blue-collar workers' or the Brits call working class.

No one on either side of the 'pond' expected someone like me to go off to a highfalutin university like the University of California at Davis and get a PhD in literature.

To make matters worse, I grew up in a part of the US that hasn't historically had the best track record on women's rights: Oklahoma. On learning I had started my PhD, one of my great-uncles (who was born in the late 1920s) asked why I hadn't found a husband when I was an undergrad (I don't have an MA, but that's a story for another time). I gave a non-committal answer and ended the conversation as quickly as I could; there was no point in trying to convince him that a PhD wasn't somehow a substitute for a husband. In the world he grew up in women got married and had children; if they did anything else in addition to that, fine, but they weren't expected to. He would be baffled by the idea that I am now writing and publishing a book to help other women write books.

All of this is to say that I know you may get some push back from people in your lives, but you shouldn't let that stop you. If you need to write your book, you should write it. If they (whoever *they* are) don't think you should, that's their problem – not yours.

I've been lucky, my immediate family have always supported my education and business. I know this isn't always the case; I've had students and clients who have had to overcome objections from parents and partners. That certainly complicates things, but it need not be the end of your journey as an author.

How you deal with such objections will often be determined by how close your relationship is with the person who objects. I don't often see my great uncle, so I just carry on doing what I want to do. When I've had professors who were prejudiced against working class students (luckily those were few and far between), I tended to work harder to show them that I was good enough.

If you live with the person (or people) who thinks you shouldn't or can't write a book, it can be harder. You'll have to set some boundaries to protect your writing time. You'll also need to spend some time trying to understand the root of their objection.

Often these objections come from a place of fear. They may fear that you won't value them after you write your book. Or that you will judge them for not having the courage to do what you are doing. Or they may simply worry that you'll be too busy for them while you write your book or if your book increases your business once it's published. They could be worried that you'll become more successful than they are.

Once you understand where the objections are coming from, you can try to mitigate them. However, you cannot let appeasing the objectors get in the way of writing your book. Ultimately their feelings about what you do or don't do are none of your business. They need to deal with their feelings; you need to deal with yours.

I know, it's easy for me to say you need to just let it go and let them have their objections. If you're living with it, it is tough. You will need support, and the best place to find that support is from other writers. In Chapter 5, 'What help might you need?', I discuss how you can find support from a variety of places, including in-person writing groups.

CHAPTER 3

HOW WILL WRITING A BOOK HELP MY BUSINESS?

CAN you run a successful business without writing a book? Of course, you can. Do you still need to write a book? Yes, I think you do.

You need to write a book for yourself, for your future clients, and for those who need to hear what you have to say but who will never work with you.

FOR YOU

I think you need to write your book for yourself because it will help you solidify a few things in your own mind:

1) You are an expert in your field;
2) You do have something to say that's worth reading;
3) You can and do help others.

There are many other benefits to writing a book, but I highlight these because they are particularly important to female entrepreneurs.

I silently cringe every time a female business owner tells me she 'just' does x, y, and z. It's time for us to stop devaluing what we do and own our expertise. You don't *just* do what you do - you do it, and you are the best at doing it your way. You bring knowledge and experience to the task that no one else does.

You need to own your expertise: the people who look up to you need to see you own it, and your customers need to see you own it. This is not something to shy away from or be embarrassed about; what you do is important, and it is important that you share it with the world.

Once you own your expertise and write your book, it will help your clients.

FOR YOUR CLIENTS

Female entrepreneurs tend to be more comfortable with helping people than with being experts. I see absolutely no reason why you can't do both: serve as an expert.

Your future clients need to read your book so they can find out how wonderful you are. This isn't to say that you'll spend the whole book shouting about how great you are, but rather that they will gather from the wealth of information you give them in the book that they need to work with you.

Not everything you do can be distilled into the text your readers will read; they know that. They also know that if what you write in your book is spectacular, what you can deliver in person will be even better.

In short, writing a book allows you to help your clients understand what they need and advertise your services to them in a distinctly un-salesy sort of way. So, while your book does work to advertise your business, it won't read as hundreds of pages of sales copy.

Instead, your book will teach your future clients something and inspire them to seek out your services.

Also, it will help your current and past clients remember what they learned from you – your book is better than any notes they may have taken at the time, because *you* have written it and *you* have checked that it is complete.

FOR OTHERS WHO NEED YOU BUT CAN'T (OR WON'T) HIRE YOU

Finally, your book is useful for those who need you but can't or won't hire you. These may be people who simply cannot afford your services, or those who are determined to figure it out on their own. These may even be people who can't hire you because they live in a different time zone and simply could never find time to actually work with you.

Whatever the reason, there are people in this world who will benefit from what you have to teach who cannot work directly with you. This is where your book comes in.

Your book is affordable, and it is available 24 hours a day, 7 days a week.

You may not be able to teach these people all they need to know in one little book, but you can show them what they need to know and point the way to finding the answers they need to find.

CHAPTER 4
WHY SHOULD YOU LISTEN TO ME ABOUT WRITING?

I'M not going to bore you with my life story here, but I will explain how I'm qualified to help you write a book.

I have a PhD in English Literature from the University of California at Davis. This is important here for two reasons: 1) since I have a PhD and you're reading this book, you know I've written a fair amount (at the very least my thesis and this book!); and 2) all English postgrads at UC Davis teach writing to undergraduates. In preparation for that teaching we undergo extensive training in how to teach writing.

I taught writing and literary studies at UC Davis for 6 years and at a couple of UK universities (Canterbury Christ Church and the University of Portsmouth) for another 6 years. That's a lot of time in classrooms working with students on their writing.

In addition to this experience, I've been working as an editor and proofreader since 2001. In this role, I've worked on a wide variety of texts from a biography about a twentieth-century Czech composer to website copy for new businesses.

I've been a member of the Chartered Institute of Editing and Proofreading, formerly the Society for Editors and Proofreaders, since 2017. Also, I've worked as a writing coach for the last several years.

All of this means that I know a lot about the writing process (both my own and my students' and clients') and about the mechanics of organising text on the page. I've worked with writers for whom English is their fourth or fifth language and writers whose brains struggle with letters and other symbols. I've helped reluctant bloggers trust what they have to say and feel confident about clicking 'publish now', and I've helped clients navigate the process of pitching their books to literary agents.

The experience and training I bring to this book mean that you can trust my advice. I'm not going to try to tell you everything I know about writing, but I will tell you what you need to know to write your book. After all, that's why you're here. You need to write your book, and your future readers need to read it!

Finally, I believe you need to write your book now. There has never been a better time to publish a book. With the advent of self-publishing, writers no longer have to get through the gatekeepers (publishers) to be heard. Also, this is the best opportunity we've ever had to balance the historical skew towards white male authors.

Don't get me wrong, I love and respect a great many white male authors (I'm married to one), but they've had their turn. It's time now for other voices to take the stage and insist on being heard. I'm here to help you be heard. Your voice needs to be out there; you need to be heard.

CHAPTER 5
WHAT HELP MIGHT YOU NEED?

BEFORE you start writing, you need to think about what kind of support you're likely to need and get it in place. You will need an editorial professional at some point. Since you'll be hiring someone to edit (copy edit, proof-edit or proofread) your book, you'll need to book them in advance. Many editors book their work months in advance. You need to keep this in mind because you simply cannot expect them to drop everything because you didn't plan well, and you 'need' your book edited now.

Some editors will take such last-minute jobs, but you will pay extra for the short notice. For example, I charge *at least* double for last minute work, on the rare occasion I'm able to take it on. More often, when I get a last-minute request, I have to tell the writer that I'm fully booked and wish them well in their search for an editor.

The same principle applies to hiring cover designers and formatters. You cannot expect people to be free and ready to work at your whim.

I'll start with the non-negotiables; these are the people you must hire if you want your book to look and feel professional to your readers (as a business owner, there's no point in writing one if you don't want this). Then, I'll discuss the nice to haves and the ones you might need.

NON-NEGOTIABLES

1) **EDITOR/PROOFREADER.** You must hire a professional (by that I mean, qualified by a nationally recognised body) proofreader/editor. I am such an editor/proofreader (I started editing and proofreading professionally in 2001), and I have hired one for this book.

   You may be asking why a qualified and experienced editor and proofreader would pay someone else to do what she's been trained to do. I hired a proofreader because it is impossible to proofread your own work.

   This is one of those cases in which you're too clever for your own good. When you read your own work, you know what you meant to say, so that's what your brain 'sees' on the page – whether it's there or not.

   You'll find a clear explanation of the different levels of editing on the website for the Chartered Institute for Editing and Proofreading (https://www.ciep.uk/about/faqs/what-is-the-difference-between-copyediting-and-proofreading/). For now, though, it is important that you understand what proofreading is and what it is not.

A proofreader catches the mistakes that are not caught in earlier rounds of editing. A proofreader does not help you with structure, focus, or coherence.

Do not skimp on this. Many of your readers will know when you've 'broken' the rules, and they may not be forgiving. For example, I once read a book by a businesswoman I happen to know and trust. The book is riddled with simple errors, and I only finished because I know her well enough to trust that what she says is worth picking out of the mistake strewn rubble. If I didn't know her, I'd have quit after chapter 1.

Will all of your readers know and trust you enough to keep reading through the irritating mistakes? If not, you absolutely must hire a professional to ensure these mistakes are few and far between.

> — Please note that any 'professional' who promises flawless copy is lying to you (and possibly to themselves).

If you can only afford one round of editing, you need a proof-edit,[1] which is more involved than proofreading (and often takes place at an earlier stage), but not as involved as copyediting.

2) **COVER DESIGNER.** You must hire a professional cover designer. The only (possible) exception to this is if you are a designer (or at least have an extensive design background).

---

[1] https://www.ciep.uk/about/faqs/what-is-proofreading/

We've all heard the cliché that 'you shouldn't judge a book by its cover'. That may be true, but people *will* judge your book by its cover. If the thumbprint cover doesn't catch your potential reader's eye when scrolling through Google or Amazon, they won't click on it to find out what it's about.

If your business book doesn't look like the kind of business book your reader is trying to find, she won't click on it to read more.

What do I mean by 'look like' the kind of book she's after? I'll use a movie to make this point. Likely, you've heard of (or even seen) the 1995 Sandra Bullock movie *While You Were Sleeping*, directed by Jon Turteltaub. When you Google this movie, the cover you are shown is of Sandra Bullock looking happily in love in the arms of Bill Pullman. The designers nailed it – the cover tells us it is a romantic drama, and that's what it is.

However, if we took the same title, *While You Were Sleeping*, and put it on a picture of Peter Gallagher's character unconscious in a hospital bed, it becomes sinister. This is especially true if you choose a 'sinister' typeface and colour. So, if the title, instead of being in yellow above the characters, was in blue, black, or red and in a larger font that covered most of the bottom of the picture, our rom-dram suddenly looks like a thriller.

This is just one of the myriad things that could go wrong in cover design. So, if you value the work you are putting into writing your book, and you want to make sure your target audience read and benefit from your book, hire a professional.

3) **BOOK FORMATTER.** Unless you are a professional book formatter, you **must** either hire one or enrol on a course to learn how to format your book. No one wants to read a book that looks like someone put it together at their kitchen table. You need someone who knows what they're doing to make sure you don't have weird gaps between paragraphs or 'orphan' sentences.

    You also need someone who understands which typefaces are best. Sorry to be the bearer of bad news, but the best one may not be your favourite one. The formatter will look at your book from the reader's perspective — at this point in the process, the only perspective that really matters is the reader's.

4) **BETA READERS.** You need beta readers to make sure you have communicated your message in a way that resonates with your target audience. I discuss this in more detail in Chapter 17, 'Beta Readers'.

Support that would be nice to have or might be necessary for some writers includes the following:

1) **A DEVELOPMENTAL EDITOR.** A developmental editor helps with big picture issues, like the overall focus and structure of the book. Such editors do not help with sentence level issues. If you're really struggling to figure out how to write your book, you may need a developmental editor's help.

2) **A WRITING COACH OR COURSE.** If you've never written a book before, you might need help with the details. A writing coach or course can help you figure out what you need to do and when you need to do it. They can also, depending on how they work, help you with accountability and motivation. You don't want to be talking about writing your book 'someday' in 10 years' time.

3) **A WRITING GROUP.** This does what it says on the tin - find a group of writers (among your friends, online, at a local library...) and get together (virtually or in person) to write. These groups will help you with motivation. They also help with the feelings of isolation that can go along with writing a book.

4) **A CRITIQUE GROUP.** Like a writing group, this is a group of writers you join (or bring together). Unlike a writing group, instead of writing during your meetings, you discuss one another's work. Every group has its own structure. Some send work to each other a few weeks before the meeting, so everyone has time to read and think about it before they meet. Others have one or two members read their work out loud to the group and then discuss it.

CHAPTER 6
GETTING STARTED

THE first step to writing a book is to choose your topic. This may sound obvious and fairly straightforward, but you need to make sure your topic is focused enough to be covered in the space of your book.

Those of you who have never written anything that's longer than a few pages will be tempted to choose a topic that is too broad. Doing this will not, contrary to what you may think, make it easier for you to write enough words. It will, in fact, make it harder for you to write any words at all.

Trying to write about a huge topic leads to paralysis - you'll find yourself staring at your computer screen not knowing where to start. Choosing a narrow topic will both make it easier to figure out where to start and easier to make sure you explain your argument clearly.

Let's take this book, for example. My broad topic is writing, but my specific topic is teaching women who own small businesses how to write their first expert book. What this won't include is how to form letters (at one end of the spectrum) or how to publish that book (at the other end of the spectrum), though Samantha Pearce from SWATT Books gives you an overview of this in the afterword to this book, or any other kind of writing. This book will have limited use, for example, to a fiction writer or an experienced nonfiction writer.

I generally tell clients to come up with what they think is a focused topic and then narrow further – and keep narrowing it until they can't narrow it any more.

STATEMENT OF ARGUMENT

Once you have your narrowly focused topic, it's time to state that topic in a single sentence: your statement of argument. This sentence will state the main point of your book and begin to answer the question every reader, consciously or not, will ask of your book: so what?

Your statement of argument needs to be an argument, not a statement of fact. This is vital because it will shape the book as a whole. If you start with a statement of fact, it won't be clear to you, or, crucially, to your reader, what the point of your book is.

If I tried to use something like 'There's a Book in Every Expert is about writing' as my statement of argument, no one would know what it was about. Is it going to explain how to form sentences, the finer points of grammar and punctuation, or something else entirely?

Try to draft a working statement of argument. My working statement is this:

> In this book, I help female coaches and healers by teaching them how to write a book that establishes their authority.

If, like I am in this book, your book seeks to teach your reader something, your statement of argument needs to say what that is (write a book) and why they would want to do that (to establish your authority).

A note about crafting this statement: while it is important, don't spend more than an hour or so working on it—this statement, like virtually everything else you write, will change and adapt over time.

OUTLINE

Once you have your focused topic, you're ready to create an outline. I don't tend to produce detailed outlines, but rather I list topics to cover in each chapter. Then, as I start each chapter, I spend some time deciding which topics to cover within it.

This works for some writers, while others will prefer spending several days at the beginning of a project outlining the book at chapter level and each chapter at section, or even paragraph, level.

If you don't instinctively have a preference, try one method; if that doesn't work, try the other. I know that this advice will read as 'wishy-washy' to the more analytically-minded amongst us, but it really is a matter of personal preference.

I can tell you what I do, but I cannot guarantee that it will work for you.

When I create the book-level outline, I put my statement of argument at the top of a new page and then ask questions of it. So, for this book I asked what a new writer would need to know and came up with questions including the following:

- Why should I write a book?
- How will it help my business?
- How do I start writing a book? - the task seems far too big
- How do I overcome writer's block?
- How do I deal with other writing obstacles?
- Where will I find the time?

As you create your list of questions, just write all of the questions that come to mind. You may find that some of them need to be combined; for example, the question about writer's block and the one about other writing obstacles should be combined. Once you have your list of questions, go through and weed out any that aren't important and combine questions as appropriate.

My one sentence answers to these questions form the statements of argument for each chapter. Then when I start a chapter, I go through the question asking process again to decide what that chapter needs to cover; the answers to those questions become the statements of argument for each section of the chapter.

At this point, I don't spend too much time thinking about the order in which to discuss things beyond the obvious. For example, for this book I need to discuss how to start your book before I discuss how to edit your first draft or when to send it to beta readers and your proofreader.

When you're happy that you have a fairly comprehensive list of chapter topics, choose one and start writing.

I like this method of outlining because if you are asking questions of your primary statement of argument, you know that you're staying on topic and not wandering off on a tangent.

CHAPTER 7

WRITE LITTLE AND OFTEN – ESPECIALLY WHEN YOU DON'T WANT TO

IF you're going to run a business, take care of yourself (family, house, pets, health...), and have a life, you need a sustainable writing practice.

Unsurprisingly, step one in creating a sustainable writing practice is committing to writing little and often. When you plan your week, where possible block out an hour or two for concentrated work. On your busier days, block out a few minutes to check in with your project.

Anyone who's experienced in project management (and writing a book is a project you need to manage) knows that blocking time in a calendar doesn't necessarily lead to work getting done. When the project in question is of a creative nature – even if you think you're writing a dry as dust instruction manual, your writing requires an element of creativity – the reasons, or excuses, for not working on it in the allotted time are usually along the lines of (cue whiney voice here) 'I don't have anything to say', 'I need to do more research', 'My sock drawer really needs to be re-organised'...

All of these excuses boil down to this: I don't want to because I don't feel inspired.

If it were quantifiable, we'd likely find that the concept of 'inspiration' has done more to rob humanity of great works of art, new inventions, and better processes for doing things than anything else, ever.

Okay, maybe I'm being a touch hyperbolic, but waiting for inspiration won't fix your writing problems. This is made clear in literature going back to ancient Greece.

Inspiration is a myth – it goes back to the Muses. The muses, as you may know, were a capricious lot who sometimes visited great artists and gave them amazing abilities, and at other times withheld their magical influence. If you rely on this sort of magical belief in inspiration, you will never finish your book.

Even writers who have written famous works about inspiration – like William Wordsworth, who wrote that poetry should be 'the spontaneous overflow of powerful feelings ... recollected in tranquillity' (p. 266) – worked at their writing.

Productive, successful writers write when it's time to write; perpetually aspiring writers wait for the mood to strike. If you're serious about writing your book, you'll choose the former.

So, what's an uninspired writer to do? Write anyway. When you have scheduled writing time, whether you're planning to work for 10 minutes or 3 hours, you must write something. If you really aren't 'feeling it' on a given day, set a timer and write about why you don't want to write for at least 10 minutes. Among academic writing coaches, this is called a ventilation file.

The ventilation file was introduced to academic writing by David Sternberg in a book called *How to Complete and Survive a Doctoral Dissertation* (1981). For a ventilation file to be useful, it needs to be for your eyes only.

Such files help you alleviate the guilt that goes with not writing when you 'should' be writing. They also help you keep the writer's block that hit you this morning from halting progress on your project for the next 6 months.

Use your ventilation file to write about why the book you're halfway through writing is suddenly 'pointless' or 'stupid'. Use it to work through any anxiety about how others will perceive your book, or even the fact that you're writing a book. Use it to tell the voice of impostor syndrome to shut up already.

You get the idea.

Some days you'll write in your ventilation file for 10 minutes, and then find that you do have something to say and get to work. Other days, you still won't be feeling it, and you'll put your writing away for the day, secure in the knowledge that you tried and will try again the following day.

And you *must* try again the next day. When we do something regularly, we stop judging it. Consider two things you probably do regularly: clean your teeth and take out the bins.

When was the last time you finished brushing your teeth or taking out the bins and thought to yourself 'I'm really rubbish at that; I must be an idiot'? I'd guess you've never thought that.

You've been brushing your teeth since you were old enough to be trusted with a toothbrush and toothpaste and taking out the bins at least since you were old enough to live on your own. It has never occurred to you to use either activity as a measure of your intelligence or self-worth.

If you start writing for at least a few minutes most days, you'll stop using writing to judge yourself - it'll be as innocuous as brushing your teeth or taking out the bins.

FINDING TIME

I'll explain this in more detail in Chapter 8, 'First Drafts', but for now it's enough to say that you'll be writing your first draft as quickly as you can to help keep your writing demons at bay - if you're writing quickly, you won't have time to worry about how your work will be received or whether you're good enough to write a book.

Though you're going to write this draft quickly, that isn't to say that you won't need to clear some significant amounts of time in your schedule for writing. Often when new writers start thinking about time to write they look to clear whole days in their schedule. I did this in the early years of my PhD.

This isn't the most efficient way to write because writing doesn't happen in 8- to 10-hour chunks of time but in 10- to 30-minute chunks.

Even when I have devoted entire days to writing, I've only managed a total of about 4 or 5 hours of actual writing. The rest of the time was frittered away on research I erroneously thought I needed to do (more on that below), or on tidying my office, doing the dishes, and organising the spice drawer. In other words, if you give yourself a day for writing, you will be setting yourself up for frustration and procrastination. However, if you schedule small writing sessions, you'll knuckle down and get to work.[2]

We've been shown to be more productive in short, focused sessions than in longer sessions. I was sceptical of this research when I first came across it, so I did a little experiment. One day, I had my usual 4 hours blocked out for writing and sat down to write. The following day, I scheduled 8 30-minute writing sessions throughout the course of the day. I used timers to keep to schedule and kept track of how many words I wrote (I was working on a first draft at the time). I wrote more than twice as many words on the second day.

---

[2] I come back to this idea in 'Managing Long Writing Sessions' (Chapter 12); if you want to read more about the research, you'll find some interesting information here: https://www.psychologytoday.com/gb/blog/intrinsic-motivation-and-magical-unicorns/201307/manage-procrastination-the-pomodoro-technique

I've since found that in 30 minutes of writing (again, on a first draft), I can usually produce about 400 words.

They aren't especially good words, and they certainly aren't polished and well organised, but they're words on a page and that's what is required of a first draft. We call first drafts rough drafts because they are supposed to be *rough*.

You may be thinking that this is all very well saying you should write in short sessions, but you need time to get in the mood and remember where you left off, and decide what you want to say and …

Let me cut you off right there. This is where breadcrumbs are helpful.

THE IMPORTANCE OF BREADCRUMBS

How can you quickly get stuck into working on your book when you only have 10 minutes, and it usually takes you 20 to get good and ready to write? Leave yourself some breadcrumbs.

Don't worry, I'm not going to suggest you sprinkle them about your workspace to clog up your keyboard. By breadcrumbs, I mean you should leave yourself a little trail to follow in the form of brief notes or an outline.

Some writers are firm believers in outlines and produce beautiful, complex, multilevel outlines before they write their first sentence. In writing jargon, these people are planners.

The rest of us are pantsers (we tend to fly by the seat of our pants) or plantsers (a hybrid writer who plans a little and then just lets loose).

I've never been able to produce detailed outlines. At school when my teacher actually assessed our outlines, I would just write the essay a few weeks early and then reverse engineer an outline to hand in.

If you're not a planner, don't worry; you don't have to be. Nevertheless, I've been a happier writer since I became a plantser. I find that spending some time thinking about the large divisions in my text (for a book, chapter headings), is useful; however, I don't bother with figuring out exactly what each chapter will cover before I write it. If even the chapter level of outlining isn't useful for you, don't do it.

If you create any sort of outline, you'll have at least the beginnings of a breadcrumb trail to follow at the beginning of each writing session. Whether you use outlines or not, you'll make your life easier if you spend a minute or two at the *end* of each session leaving yourself a few notes (or breadcrumbs) on what you mean to write next. This will allow you to quickly get back into your train of thought and make meaningful progress on your project in even a few minutes.

Remember that the notes you leave at the end of a session shouldn't be elaborate; a few bullet points of where you need to go next in what you've been working on will suffice.

THE IMPORTANCE OF RITUAL

The brain loves routine and ritual. There's a reason sleep experts advise us to develop bedtime routines – when you do the same things in the same order every time, your brain comes to expect the desired outcome. So, if you have a cup of herbal tea and read a chapter of a book before brushing your teeth and going to bed, your brain will associate the activity of drinking that particular tea with getting ready to sleep. After a few nights, you'll find yourself nodding off more easily than before.

The same is true of other routines. If you write to music, make a writing play list. If you always write in one particular spot, keep that spot just for writing, as far as possible. You could even develop habits like putting on a sweater, lighting a candle, or making a cup of coffee in a special mug at the start of each writing session. Any small, pleasant thing you can do at the beginning of each session will help you get into your writing more quickly.

This kind of mood setting, as opposed to waiting for inspiration to strike, works because you are in control of it.

WHAT IF I JUST CAN'T?

These tips and techniques will work just fine for the vast majority of your writing sessions. But what do you do on those days when your brain will just not cooperate? When you go through your routine, sit down and try to write and nothing happens, there are several things you could do, but which one will work best depends on what's causing the resistance.

If you're struggling to write because you're exhausted after a night of broken sleep because the cat had a hairball at two in the morning and you couldn't get back to sleep afterwards because of your husband's snoring, the solution is clear - you need to rest.

If you're hesitating to write because you need to do more research, spend your writing time making a *focused* list of questions you need to find answers to. You need this list and you need it to be focused to help you not use research as an excuse not to write. There will always be more to learn, and you will never know everything there is to know about your topic; you just need to know enough to help your reader.

Once you have a list of things you genuinely need to research, make a plan for how and when you're going to find that information. Then, just as you've scheduled your writing in short sessions, do the same with your research. If, for example, you determine you need to read a recently published book in your field, once you obtain a copy, plan time to read it. But don't approach this the way you would approach reading a novel for fun. You're reading for information here. Keep a notebook nearby with the list of things you need to know for your writing - you're not taking the kinds of notes you would take if you were to sit an exam on the book, but the kind of notes you need for your writing. Also, every couple of chapters (or every chapter if they're very long or dense), spend a few minutes writing about how you can incorporate what you've read into your book – taking care to cite all paraphrases and quotations.

Making yourself pause to write about what you're reading will help you stay focused on the important thing – your book.

If you're struggling to write because of anxiety over writing itself, turn to Chapter 9, 'Writer's Block, Impostor Syndrome, and Other Things that Keep Writers Up at Night'.

HOW LONG SHOULD IT BE?

There really isn't a satisfying answer to this since the answer is, as long as it needs to be to cover your topic.

If you're writing your book to introduce people to your business – the sort of book you'd give away in a lead magnet – you'll only need 10,000 to 20,000 words.

If you're writing to both introduce people to what you do and to teach them something – the kind of book you would sell – you'll need 30,000 to 50,000 words. The best way to decide how long you want your book to be is to look at how long books like yours are.

Pick up one or two of your favourites and work out a rough word count. You can do this by counting how many words are in each of three lines of text; take the average; then multiply this by how many lines of text are on a page. You then multiply this by how many pages are in the book – since there will be blank lines/pages and may be illustrations, this is only a rough estimate, but it's close enough for your purposes. Keep these examples of good practice handy - you'll need them when you revise to help you decide things like how many chapters you really need and how long each chapter should be.

CHAPTER 8
FIRST DRAFTS

NOW that you have a topic and an outline, it's time to start writing. This is both the most exciting and the scariest part of any writing project.

To make this process more productive and enjoyable, I want you to hold on to the excitement and ignore the fear.

Your first draft is just that: a draft.

You are likely the only person who will ever read your first draft, so don't worry about niggly little details like word choice, sentence structure, or exactly where you need commas and semicolons.

As you write the first draft, I want you to write as quickly as possible. This is a tried and tested method for writing first drafts. Anne Lamott discusses it in *Bird by Bird* (1995), and the concept forms the basis of National Novel Writing Month (NaNoWriMo). If you haven't heard of NaNoWriMo, it takes place every November; thousands of writers commit to writing 50,000 words in 30 days. To learn more about it, see Chris Baty's *No Plot? No Problem* (2014).

For the first draft of your book, it is important to write quickly because you need to finish it as soon as possible.

If you let yourself slow down, you'll get bogged down in details that don't matter at this stage, and you'll risk opening the door for some nasty writing demons.

Since I touch type with reasonable accuracy, I like to write first drafts on my laptop while sitting in cafés or on trains. As I typed the first draft of this sentence, I was on a train to Birmingham; I kept my pace up by watching the scenery outside the window while typing away. If I have to write on a desktop or in a place where I don't have scenery or people to watch, I recreate this by turning off the monitor. Yes, there will be typos when I return to the text, but the time it takes to sort those is minuscule compared to the time saved by getting a lot of words down quickly.

Why does writing without looking speed things up? It makes it easier for you to ignore your internal editor. You're freer to make mistakes in settings where you accept that mistakes are unavoidable. Thus, I don't waste time trying to find the perfect word; instead, I just write. In short, you can't edit what you can't see.

SETTING DEADLINES FOR YOUR FIRST DRAFT

To further 'block proof' your writing practice, you need to be clear from the outset what counts as writing. When you write your first draft, you should write as quickly as possible without worrying about things like spelling, sentence structure, or the larger structure of your book.

Whether you're writing a novel or a book about how to change the oil in a '69 Mustang, the purpose of the first draft is to dump your ideas onto the page. If you take your time over the first draft, you aren't going to produce a better draft, you're just going to take longer to produce a shitty draft. No, I don't mean to insult your first draft; all first drafts are shit, as Ernest Hemingway is supposed to have said. Run a search for "shitty first drafts" (include the speech marks), and you'll find a chapter by that name from Anne Lamott's *Bird by Bird*.

As Lamott makes clear, a shitty first draft is not only *not* a problem, it's a requirement. We all have to write a rough draft before we can polish it into anything better.

When you start writing your first draft, you will probably measure your progress in terms of how many hundreds of words you write each day. For a first draft, that's fine. For second and subsequent drafts, you'll feel discouraged when you record that not only did you not add any words, you actually cut a few hundred! So, after you finish your first draft, choose another way to track your progress, such as sections edited.

This is important, so I'll say it again: in your first draft, adding words = progress. For all other drafts, find a different way to measure progress.

As you write your first draft, keep track of how long each session is and how many words you write in each session. After a few days, you'll have a good idea of how many words you can write in an hour; this will give you a realistic idea of how much time you need to set aside to write your first draft.

For example, I know that I can write about 800 words an hour; so, I'll need 50 hours to write a 40,000-word book. Since I need to fit my writing in around everything else (editing work, coaching sessions, workshops, work on growing my business, normal life stuff, and having a social life), I know that I don't want to commit to more than about 15 hours a week. This means I'll need roughly one month to write my first draft. We'll come back to other uses for your words per hour rate in the next section.

You need to work out your finish date early in the process for a couple of reasons. First, having a finish date means you can tell others when you're planning to finish - this is the best motivation you can get, and accountability is necessary for long projects like writing a book.

Second, you need to know when you'll have a draft so you can work out when you'll need to have an editor and your beta readers work on your draft. You can't expect that an editor will be free when you want her to be - so choose your editor and schedule the work before you start your draft.

If money is tight, find a friend who writes well to act as your first editor; even though this is likely to be done as a favour, you still need to give this person some idea of when you'll send them the manuscript.

Likewise, If you're asking your beta readers to take no more than a month to read the draft and get back to you with their feedback, you need to let them know when you'll send them the manuscript. Also, putting these things in place before you start writing will act as further incentive to keep going.

If you're now thinking, but I thought you said no one else would read my first draft - I did. You're not going to send them your first draft. In Chapters 15 and 16, I explain how you're going to make your manuscript as good as it can be before you send it to your editor or beta readers.

SETTING GOALS

We need goals. When I sit down to write and just have a vague idea of how long I'll write, I often end up spending a lot of time on social media, tidying my desk, and entertaining my cat. When I sit down to write 1,000 words of the rough draft I'm working on, I write 1,000 words. Similarly, if I block out time to revise a particular chapter, I crack on with that without procrastinating.

To set goals that are helpful, you need to remember a few things.

- Your goals need to be specific and measurable. If you don't know what you're aiming for, you won't know when you've hit it.
- They need to be achievable.
- You need session goals and larger ones; both kinds should be achievable.
- Your goals need to have an endpoint, and you need to track them in a way that is meaningful for you.

This is probably starting to sound familiar. If you've spent any time reading about goal setting in the last several years, you'll have come across the idea of SMART goals. These are Specific, Measurable, Achievable, Realistic, and Time bound (there are other versions; they all make the same point, so use the one you like best). The important point here isn't choosing and remembering an acronym but making sure you've set a goal that you can actually reach.

As I said above, your goals need to be specific and measurable; this is important because if your goal is unclear or hazy, you won't know when you've reached it.

Your goals also need to be realistic. While it's good to set goals that stretch you, if your goal is impossible, you'll just get frustrated and quit. This is why you need to set achievable, realistic goals. Your goals need to come with deadlines, otherwise they will just always be out there somewhere in the future. Deadlines inspire action.

This is all well and good in the abstract, but how will it look for you in practice? In the beginning, it will be hard for you to set specific goals. Once you have your words per hour rate, you'll have a reasonable number of words to aim for in each session.

For example, when I'm writing on a topic I know well, like this one, I know that I can produce 800 to 1200 words an hour. I've been writing for a long time and know that I write quickly. I also know that I've already developed the practice of writing without editing. If you're still trying to silence your inner editor, you'll write more slowly (though with practice you'll speed up). So, if you average 600 words an hour, you know that at the beginning of a 10-minute writing block, you'll need to aim to produce 100 words. Having this in mind will help you quiet your inner editor and keep you from procrastinating.

In addition to goals for individual writing sessions, you will also need some bigger goals. We've looked at how to use your words per hour rate to set the deadline for your first draft. Review that deadline and make sure it actually works for your life (not just in theory).

For instance, I determined that I could write a 40,000-word draft in 4 weeks because I can comfortably write 2,000 words a day 5 days a week. I may be a more experienced writer than you are (and have a correspondingly faster writing rate), and I know I have fewer caring responsibilities than many of you (I live with my husband and our cat; they're both fairly self-sufficient). When you're setting your big goal, make sure you take your whole life into account, not just your business life.

Repeat this process with your second and subsequent drafts, but then you'll use how many pages you can edit per hour to arrive at your estimate.

In addition to the big goals of finishing each draft, you'll need monthly (if your work will be spread over multiple months) and weekly goals. These are important to keep you on track. It's all too easy early in a project to fall behind and tell yourself you'll catch up later. Doing this frequently leads to frantic work nearer to the deadline and/or a missed deadline. Having these benchmarks will help keep you on track.

When you're planning your week, you can also look at setting provisional daily goals during the week. We all know that in business, if it's not in the diary it doesn't get done - schedule your writing sessions and make a note of what you plan to do in each. Then, each day, look at your progress and what you have planned and revise your daily goal as needed.

For example, if your writing goal for the day is to write 1,000 words on a particular topic and you have three sessions of varying lengths, take a minute to break the goal down into parts you can manage in each of your sessions. Having three smaller goals will make it easier for you to focus in each of your sessions. Write down each of these in your diary; for example, if my goal were to write 1,000 words on goal setting and I had three sessions, I'd plan to write about 500 words on smart goals, 300 on large, long-term goals, and 200 on daily goals. Looking at my diary and seeing 'write 300 words on large, long-term goals' in the block of time after lunch is going to be more motivating than seeing 'write'. That said, don't try to plan at this level too far in advance (especially when you're working on your first draft), because you don't really know what you'll need to write in a particular session until you're closer to the time.

CHAPTER 9
WRITER'S BLOCK, IMPOSTOR SYNDROME, AND OTHER THINGS THAT KEEP WRITERS UP AT NIGHT

ALL writers occasionally experience what I call *writing demons*. I've yet to find a writer with a reliable way of vanquishing them, but I have gathered tips and tricks for taming them over the years.

In this chapter, I'll discuss some well-known demons like writer's block, impostor syndrome, and perfectionism. These demons are similar to one another like a close-knit, obnoxious family. For this reason, there will be some overlap in my advice for dealing with each. If you're reading this chapter through from beginning to end, you'll just have to skim material that has been covered in a previous section. I'm intentionally leaving the repetition in so that if you return to the book when you're having a particular problem, it will be easy for you to find the tip you're looking for without rereading the whole chapter; I know you don't have time for that.

WRITER'S BLOCK

Writer's block is likely the best known and most common problem faced by writers. A blocked writer is one who knows she has something to say, but for whatever reason, isn't able to put words on the page. Writer's Block likes bringing Perfectionism along for added fun, so if you're having this problem make sure you look at both sections.

This demon's favourite time to strike is when your writing has been sailing along smoothly for days or even weeks; then, all of a sudden, you can't write at all.

This is not cause for panic; you haven't suddenly lost the ability to string words together - I'm not a betting woman, but even I'd bet you were still able to speak to friends and family even on your most blocked day, and odds are you're still able to do other kinds of writing like simple emails or notes to put in your kid's lunchbox.

It's this odd quirk that a blocked writer can still use language, just not for 'the book', that prompts writers like Seth Godin to say things like this:

> No one ever gets talker's block. No one wakes up in the morning, discovers he has nothing to say and sits

> quietly, for days or weeks, until the muse hits, until the moment is right, until all the craziness in his life has died down.
>
> Why then, is writer's block endemic? (https://seths.blog/2011/09/talkers-block/)

That quotation, taken out of context, can sound dismissive of writer's block. I'm not suggesting it's a made-up condition; I'm simply reminding you that you can still use language, so all is not lost.

Godin goes on to suggest you 'write poorly, in public, until you can write better'. I'm not a fan of publishing work that hasn't been edited (big surprise!). You can, though, take a cue from Godin; if writing your book isn't happening on a particular day, try talking about what you're writing into to the dictation app you likely have on your phone. This will keep you focused on the task at hand, making progress on your book, while taking the pressure off the act of writing.

If you're not in a situation where talking to your phone is possible, change your writing conditions in some other way. If you usually write at the computer, change to pen and paper (or vice versa). If that doesn't work, try writing with crayon on unlined paper (extra points if the paper is a pretty, bright colour) – if you're really blocked, take your colouring to the floor like you did when you were a kid.

I particularly like the crayon/unlined paper technique. Getting rid of the lines on the page frees the mind – you're no longer bound by the conventions of producing linear text. Using crayons and bright paper further stimulates your creativity; after all, can you really judge anything you write in purple crayon on pink paper?

Another option is to change where you write; if you usually work in your home office, move to the sitting room or a café. If you usually write in a café, either try a new one or go home to write.

If you don't write to music, try putting some on; if you do, try a different genre or switch it off. During my PhD, I could only write to Mozart's Requiem Mass – it took me a while not to see that as some sort of unconscious judgement on my thesis, but I had to go with it because it worked. Mozart generally works well for intellectual work, and scientists have shown that our brainwaves line up in a more orderly way when we listen to his music than to other kinds – it's something to do with how carefully structured the pieces are; even those without musical training sense the order in the music.[3]

You could try taking a short exercise break. Physical movement not only gets your blood pumping, it also frees your mind. Rhythmic, repetitive exercise is especially good for writer's block: think walking or swimming laps. It's not an accident that famous writers are also famous walkers: Charles Dickens wandered the streets of London as much for inspiration as to overcome writer's block; Alfred, Lord Tennyson famously walked all over the Isle of Wight when he lived at Farringford; and Marianne Evans (George Eliot) walked every morning after her first work session of the day.

---

[3] For an example of a scientific study on this, see 'The Mozart Effect: A Quantitative EEG Study' (https://www.ncbi.nlm.nih.gov/pubmed/26036835)

Whatever activity you choose it needs to be engaging enough that you can't ruminate on your perceived 'failure' to write, but not so all engrossing that your brain can't keep working on the problem in the background.

The human brain is a marvellous thing, and it will keep chipping away at a problem when you're not consciously aware of it. That's why my final suggestion is to take a nap. When you've been writing for a while, you'll notice that you feel 'more inspired' first thing in the morning or after a nap. This isn't really the kind of magical inspiration I warned against in Chapter 7, 'Write Little and Often'; rather, it's evidence that your brain kept working on your book while you were asleep. How cool is that?

As you've no doubt gathered, dealing with writer's block requires changing your routine and situation enough that you can break through the block. Be creative and find what works for you.

IMPOSTOR SYNDROME, AKA THE IMP

Impostor syndrome is when you convince yourself that you're not good enough, smart enough, or in some other way not enough to write your book.

If you're reading this book, you probably have a business; whether you're wildly successful or not, you know how to do something that most other people need help with. That means that you, as you are right this minute, are enough. You *can* write your book, and it *will* help your readers.

If The Imp is in your head telling you what you can't do, you need to learn to shut it up. In her Tedx talk on the subject, Lou Solomon (https://youtu.be/whyUPLJZljE) gives her negative voice a name and then puts her in her place. If you don't want to give The Imp a name, just call it The Imp. Either way, you need to learn to talk back when it tells you you're not enough.

One very effective way of doing this is to focus on the necessary roughness of the rough draft. Writing a book, like clearing out your wardrobe, requires making a big mess before you can start to put things in order again.

So, just as a good clear out starts with throwing all your clothes on the bed and all your shoes on the floor, writing a rough draft starts with throwing all your words and ideas at the page.

Sticking with the wardrobe analogy for a minute; you wouldn't expect to be able to see coordinated outfits in the huge pile of clothes in the middle of the bed. However, this doesn't make you panic. Instead, you calmly pick up piece after piece sorting them by season, colour, or type until you've imposed enough order to start making sense of it all. Only after the initial sorting do you start deciding what to keep, what to mend, and what to donate. When you finish that round, then you look at what goes with what. By the end of the process, you'll likely find that you have several 'new' outfits you never knew you had.

The same goes for writing; the first draft is just moving all the words out of your head and onto the page. Then you start sorting and making sense of them. If you embrace this system, it will be very difficult for The Imp to take hold.

It won't be able to say, 'Who do you think you are to publish a book?' because you're not publishing a book - you're moving words from your head to the page. Several drafts later, when you get to the point of hitting publish, you will feel so accomplished that you won't even hear The Imp if it tries to interfere!

PERFECTIONISM

This demon comes in two forms: one slows your progress down to a snail's pace and the other stops you in your tracks.

Either way, it tries to make you believe that what you're writing right now is what is going to go out into the world, so it had better be perfect the first time - with the implication that something horrible will happen if it's not. It will try to rationalise this by telling you that you're really saving time by slowing down now - think of all the time you'll have when you're not working on the second or subsequent draft.

Perfectionism is a liar when it talks to writers of first drafts.

Unless your goal is to irritate your reader, the first draft is never the final draft (neither is the second or third draft, for that matter). The idea that a 'true artist' or a 'real writer' doesn't need to produce draft after draft has been with us for a long time. It goes all the way back to the Greeks with Athena springing fully formed from Zeus's head.

You wouldn't expect a newborn to get a job and be a productive member of society, so don't expect your first draft to be your final draft.

Though we've established you can't trust Perfectionism when you're writing your rough draft, it will be useful in later drafts; Perfectionism is the internal editor you'll need when it's time to revise your draft.

How do you silence Perfectionism long enough to write your first draft? In part, by writing as quickly as you can. This is why I advocate writing your first draft as quickly as possible.

If simply trying to write as quickly as you can type doesn't work, you could take this to the extreme and try freewriting for 10 to 15 minutes. When you freewrite, you type whatever comes into your head without trying to stay focused on a particular topic. Think of it as a way to record your stream of consciousness.

If you sit down to freewrite, set a timer and then write (or type) without stopping until the timer goes off. If you run out of things to say, just repeat the last word you wrote until you find something else to move on to. If this means you write the same word over and over again for 8 of your 10 minutes, so be it. Incidentally, I've never heard of anyone getting that stuck - after a few repetitions your brain will move on to something else, if for no other reason than it is bored.

When my clients exhibit deep-seated perfectionist tendencies, I suggest that they freewrite for 10 minutes a day, every day for at least a month. This helps them learn to mute the perfectionist voice while they make progress on their first draft.

THE PERPETUAL RESEARCHER

This is a particularly annoying writing demon; it seems to mean well - if you want your book to be the best that it can be, you do need to do some research. The problem is that if you always need to read just one more book or another handful of articles before you start writing, you'll never start *writing*.

If you are writing about what you do in your business and you've been doing that thing for a while, you know enough to make a good start. I'm not saying don't do any research along the way, but don't fall into the trap of thinking you have to know absolutely everything before you can even start.

To keep research in its place, start writing. As you find topics that you need to learn more about, make a note. While I wrote the first draft of this book I used {{ find …}} to mark anything I needed to look up. This way, when I took a research day, I could use the search function in Word (ctrl+f) and look for {{; I then researched the items one at a time, filling out that section of the draft as I found the information that I needed.

Most of this research won't require reading whole books, or even chapters. If you do find that you need to read a whole book, which you would do if someone published an important new book in your field, you'll need to find time to do that. As I explained in 'Write Little and Often' (Chapter 7), as you read, pause every chapter or three to write about how what you're reading needs to be incorporated into your book. Remember to cite all quotations and paraphrased passages as you take these notes; see 'Respecting Intellectual Property' (Chapter 21) for guidance on how to do that. I don't want to terrify you, but failure to cite your sources will at the very least call your integrity into question and at worst could see you in court over intellectual property theft.

FEAR OF (POSSIBLE) FUTURE CRITICISM

Some writers stop writing because they fear how others will respond to their work. When you're not in the grip of this fear, hopefully you can see that it's a bit silly to fear criticism from someone, likely a stranger, who might possibly dislike part of your book someday. When you're in the grip of it, though, it can be debilitating.

So, what's a writer to do? This demon is closely related to Perfectionism, so it should come as no surprise that you manage it in the same way. Take your writing one step at a time. Remind yourself, repeatedly, that the first draft is supposed to be a mess – all the best first drafts are.

Also, start talking back to the fear. Let's say the voice is right and a future critic doesn't like part of your book – let's take this to the highest sort of criticism a book can get: a reviewer for the *London Review of Books* doesn't like what you do in chapter 4 but is happy with the rest of the book.

This is when you would hopefully have a friend or writing coach on speed dial who could point out (repeatedly if need be) that first, your book was reviewed in *LRB*!!! That's huge! And second: the reviewer liked chapters 1 through 3 and 5 through 8.

Book reviewers aren't paid to be nice and some seem to feel compelled to find fault with at least one part of every book they review. Your other critics will function the same way. As a writer, you have to be prepared for this kind of feedback.

If someone raises a valid point that could improve your next book, or the next edition of the current one, great! Take the constructive criticism on board. However, if the critic doesn't get what you were trying to do or is just having a go at you, feel free to ignore them. It's not your job to make them happy. For more on coping with criticism, see 'Dealing with Criticism' (Chapter 19).

CHAPTER 10
CLEARING YOUR HEAD

SOMETIMES your busy brain won't want to cooperate when it's time to write. You'll need to develop techniques for clearing your head so you can carry on with your work. How you do this will depend on your mood, personality, and environment, as well as what exactly is distracting you at the moment.

If you're in a co-working space or a public place like a café, try something quiet, like deep breathing exercises. You can simply close your eyes and breathe in and out slowly. If you feel odd about sitting with closed eyes in public, look at a picture of something calming on your computer or phone screen. If simply breathing slowly doesn't work, try breathing in for 3 counts, holding it for 4, and breathing out for 5.

Wherever you're working, you could try putting on headphones and listening to a short, guided meditation or some calming music. There are several apps you could use for this, as well as several YouTube videos you can access (if you have internet access).

If you're working where it would be appropriate and you have the space for it, you could do a short yoga or stretching routine. Both of these have been shown to help quiet the mind.

As I discussed in 'Write Little and Often' (Chapter 7), you could also use your writing routine to help clear your mind. This is particularly useful if you're consistently distracted when you try to write. A routine will signal to your mind that it's time to write. Find something simple that you can do each time you write to develop this routine. Examples include lighting a candle, putting on a sweater, making a cup of tea in a special writing mug, or listening to a particular play list.

Finally, if you're struggling to focus because you keep worrying about the rest of your to-do list while you're trying to write, keep a notebook next to you while you write so you can jot down any unrelated things that pop into your head. Once you've written these down, you won't have to worry about forgetting them and should find it easier to focus. Alternatively, if the thing you're fixated on can be completed quickly, go do it and get back to your writing.

CHAPTER 11
THE IMPORTANCE OF BOUNDARIES

ONE of the best pieces of writing advice I've ever come across had to do with what to do at the end of each writing session: put it all away in a box or bag.

Putting the project away will make it easier for you to be more present in the rest of your life. It will also make the project of writing a book seem less all consuming. Even if you write on your computer, you'll likely end up with a lot of writing related stuff like books, notes, and papers. These can easily take over your working space. Since many small-business owners work, at least sometimes, in our homes, leaving the book out can make it seem like we never take time off work.

Putting the book away will make it easier for you to carry on with work in and on your business, as well as with living your life. Having it all stored away somewhere will also keep the book from encroaching on your sleep. If looking at it one more time just before you go to bed means getting it out, you probably won't do it (this is a good thing - you don't need book-induced insomnia).

If most of your book is stored on your computer and you use your computer for both work and play, keep the book files in separate folders. You'll then need to be disciplined enough not to open them when you're not working.

Clearly, putting away your book when you're not working will have benefits for you and for anyone you share your space with. If the book is in its place, you won't have to clear it off the dining table at dinner time, and when the kids spill a drink on the coffee table, it won't get on your book! In a shared office, clearing it away will help you not annoy your officemates.

If you have your own office, it's still a good habit to get into. If you're writing a book about your business, you have other work to do in your workspace. Keeping the book in its place will help you work more efficiently on other projects.

Finally, the act of taking your book stuff out of its bag or box can form part of your writing routine. This simple act will signal to your brain that it's time to write (this is why it's so dangerous to get it out just before bed).

WHAT IF THE BOOK WON'T STAY IN ITS PLACE?

We all know that it's one thing to keep the book stuff physically in its place, but that doesn't necessarily mean that your mind won't wander back to it when you're trying to do something else.

Try keeping a writer's notebook. This can take the form of a little notebook that fits easily in your pocket or handbag, or it can be the notes app on your smartphone.

Whatever method you choose, please only choose one. If you take notes in multiple formats, it's easier to misplace them. You don't want to waste your valuable writing time searching for a note!

Once you've chosen a method, keep it with you and ready to use. This way, if you're peeling potatoes and a good idea pops into your head, you can quickly jot it down and get back to making dinner. The next day, when it's time to write, you'll look at the note and, if it's still as brilliant as it seemed the night before, put it to use in your book. If you're like me, your best random ideas will come to you at the most inconvenient times (in the shower or while driving). If this happens, you'll just have to remember it until it is safe and practical to record it.

CHAPTER 12

MANAGING LONG WRITING SESSIONS

ON days that you work your writing in around everything else, you're unlikely to have a writing session that lasts for more than an hour – and most of them will be 30 minutes or shorter. For these short sessions, it's easy to stay focused.

On the relatively rare occasion that you are able to clear a day or half a day for writing, you'll need to have a game plan. Otherwise, you'll get to the end of the day and find you have little to show for it.

For longer writing sessions, I encourage writers to use the pomodoro method. This was invented by Francesco Cirillo and is named after his kitchen timer, which was shaped like a tomato, or in Italian a pomodoro.

When you use the pomodoro method, you break your time into 25-minute sessions with 5-minute breaks. A 25-minute session is one pomodoro. After 4 pomodoros (2 hours), you take a longer break of 10 to 20 minutes.

When you start a session that is going to be governed by the pomodoro system, you need to plan out what you want to do and break it into sections that can be completed in a single pomodoro. If this isn't possible, estimate how many pomodoros you'll need for a task.

At the beginning of each pomodoro, look at your list and choose one task to focus on. When you use this method for writing your first draft, you'll find that you write more words in one pomodoro than you do in one hour when you aren't using the method. This technique helps to focus the mind on a single task.

Doing one thing at a time will make you more efficient. But if thoughts of other things you need to do creep in, make a note of them on a separate sheet of paper and get back to work. Your job for 25 minutes is to focus on a single task, not to worry about everything else that's going on.

During the 5-minute breaks, you can do things like get a drink, take a comfort break, and find out what's happening on social media. During the longer break, it is important that you get up and move around.

As I'm sure you've heard, the human body needs to move. We are not meant to sit at computers all day. So, during your longer break, if it's nice outside, go for a quick walk. If it's not, do something else like a short yoga practice or walk up and down your stairs.

The point is to get the blood circulating and give the mind a chance to really relax.

CHAPTER 13
FINDING YOUR VOICE

I started my business and wrote this book because I'm passionate about helping entrepreneurs (especially female entrepreneurs) find their voice. In one sense this simply means helping you believe in your right to speak and be heard. In another, it refers to how you present yourself and your ideas.

You may never have given much thought to authorial voice, but I'm sure you've noticed it on some level when reading. Authorial voice refers to the tone an author takes when writing.

Many writing guides will suggest that you just 'write how you speak'. This is excellent advice, so far as it goes.

THE THESAURUS

The best part about the 'write how you speak' advice is that it encourages writers to use their own words. This means that you do not need to memorise a dictionary or consult a thesaurus when writing.

The thesaurus is particularly dangerous. My favourite writing teacher, the late Lawrence Frank, said the only good way to use a thesaurus was as a door stop or for kindling when lighting a fire. Now that most of us only have access to the many thesauri online or the synonyms function in Word, they serve no purpose at all.

Writers generally turn to the thesaurus when they think they don't sound smart enough and want a bigger or better word for what they're trying to say. Your readers want to hear your voice, not that of the thesaurus. If you are genuinely concerned that your vocabulary isn't big enough, read more. You'll learn new words as you read. More importantly, you'll learn how to use those words correctly.

THE DANGERS OF HUMOUR AND SARCASM

When you're writing, you'll need to be careful if your usual speech is full of jokes and sarcasm. These are great in conversation, when your audience have the benefit of body language and tone of voice to help them understand your meaning. On paper, however, they can be dangerous.

This is because you don't really intimately know each one of your readers. You have some idea of who your ideal reader is, but you cannot control who buys your book, nor can you control how they react to reading it. Also, in writing, you aren't there to gauge your audience's reaction or to immediately apologise if you cross a line. Be very, very careful with any attempt at humour.

DON'T OFFEND YOUR READER, UNLESS THAT'S YOUR POINT

Also, you'll need to be careful either to use inclusive, polite language or to announce early in the book that you won't be doing so. Several books I've read lately have included a short 'warning' that the author writes how she speaks and occasionally uses profanity. This warning may make a few potential buyers decide not to buy the book, but that's better than having them buy it only to be annoyed that they 'wasted' their money.

Inclusivity in other senses, however, is not negotiable. Unless your purpose is to offend your readers, you'll need to be sensitive to your use of pronouns and any assumptions you make about gender identity or sexual orientation. You'll need the same sensitivity when discussing issues related to race or class.

Please note that even if your book is not about gender, sexuality, race, or class, whatever you're writing about will be informed by your experience of these things. You cannot expect everyone to have had your experience, so be kind to your readers and don't exclude those who are not you.

BLACK TIE OR BUSINESS CASUAL?

A less fraught, but no less important, thing to consider is how formal you want to sound. Are you going to use contractions, or always spell everything out?

When you consider how formal you want to be, you also need to ask whether you're going to address your reader as an equal or a subordinate. This is important here because choosing a more formal tone, will come with the risk of sounding like you're lecturing at your reader or talking down to them.

I always recommend addressing your reader as an equal. Failure to do so can come off as rude and standoffish. You don't want to alienate your reader before they've got far enough to understand what you're trying to say.

If you're writing about a topic that you feel might be very familiar, and thus bleeding obvious, to some of your readers, preface that section with a statement that you're going to assume it's new to them. If that's not the case they can quickly skim the section and move on to the next, as I do at the beginning of Chapter 21, 'Respecting Intellectual Property'.

CHAPTER 14
KEEPING UP THE MOMENTUM

YOUR first few days of working on a book are likely fuelled by adrenaline and excitement. By day 3 or 4, you may feel like you've hit a wall - a very solid, seemingly unscalable wall.

Don't fret when this happens. You've been through this before. Remember the end of the first week of January, when your New Year's resolution suddenly felt unachievable? Or the last fitness regime you tried to adopt that went really well until the third workout when your body just stopped cooperating?

In battling through those struggles, you may have found ways to motivate yourself. Find a way to adapt that to this situation.

If you feel you've never battled through, or you just want another idea for self-motivation, I'll tell you in this chapter how I maintain momentum on writing projects.

It's really simple: reward yourself for writing.

Of course, at the end of the project, you'll have a book launch party. And you'll probably have some sort of celebration when you send the final draft to be published.

These are brilliant, and you should definitely celebrate your big wins.

You also need to celebrate all the little steps that get you to the end. Every time you keep a writing appointment with yourself, you need a reward. Every time you meet a word count or editing goal, you need a reward. Every time you send your document to a reader (editor, beta reader, or other), you need a reward.

This may sound like a lot of rewards, but it works. People respond better to positive reinforcement than to threats of punishment. Use that to your, and your book's, advantage.

WHAT KINDS OF REWARDS? I CAN'T HAVE A PARTY EVERY NIGHT!

Scale your rewards to fit the effort required to reach the goal you're rewarding yourself for reaching.

For example, I know one writer who absolutely loves jelly baby sweets. If she needs to write 1,000 words, she lines up 10 jelly babies on her desk and has 1 for every 100 words she writes.

A reward for keeping a scheduled writing appointment could be a nice cup of tea or a short break to read the next chapter in the novel you're reading.

You'll need bigger rewards, like a nice dinner or night out, for bigger achievements like finishing a draft. And, of course, a party for finishing the book and launching it.

HOW WILL REWARDS MOTIVATE ME?

Rewards work by making you pause, at least long enough to pop a sweet in your mouth, to acknowledge the progress you've made - this will trigger feel-good chemicals in your brain.

When we do something good and get a reward for it, we tend to want to do more good things because we want both the reward and the feel-good chemicals. The key to making this work is two-fold: choosing the right reward for you and planning the rewards in advance.

CHOOSE THE RIGHT REWARD

Choosing the right reward for you is crucial. Jelly babies work for my writer friend who loves them. I'm not so keen and would rather avoid eating them. I would, however, happily work for M&Ms. Another writer friend doesn't like sweets or chocolate at all; for her something like crisps would work better. Clearly, this is not a one size fits all situation.

My coaching clients always love the 'how will you reward yourself' conversation, and they especially love the homework: planning their rewards.

PLANNING IS EVERYTHING

Planning your rewards is as important as the rewards themselves. When you plan your rewards, you're not only making plans to treat yourself, you're also making plans to make real progress on your book.

When you plan to make progress, you solidify in your mind the idea that you are going to finish this project. When this idea is linked to fun rewards, you get excited about doing the work you need to do to finish the project.

Do yourself a favour, take some time to plan your rewards. Have fun with this but try not to make all of them sugary treats - I assume you want to keep your teeth and your health. Here's a list of suggestions, but please, add your own:

- Make yourself a nice cup of tea
- Have a fancy coffee from a café
- Enjoy a piece of cake
- Have a piece of candy
- Go for a walk outside
- Take a yoga class
- Take a nap
- Take a bath
- Buy yourself a decadent chocolate truffle for keeping all of your writing appointments for a week

- Do your nails
- Call a friend for a chat
- Get a massage
- Read a good book
- Go out for dinner
- Order takeaway
- Go to a movie
- Have a party
- Take a holiday

CHAPTER 15
FIRST REVISION

YOU'VE finished your first draft; well done! Take some time to rest and celebrate. You need this time to recover and to get some emotional distance from your writing. After a few days or a week, you'll be ready to start your first revision.

First, let's talk about what this revision is *not*. You are not sorting out sentence level issues like word choice or comma placement. This detailed level of polishing comes last.

You'll need to print your whole manuscript for this. Don't print on both sides of the page and make sure the whole thing is double spaced. In Word, you can easily do this by using ctrl+a to select the whole document and then change the spacing. Finally, before you press print, make sure each chapter begins on a new page. These details are important, because you may need to literally cut and paste sections of your draft.

I don't like wasting paper any more than you do,[4] but you need to be able to see the whole thing at once. You need to

---

[4] After you've published your book, you can take the pages that don't have notes on the back and cut them in half or quarters to turn into useful scratch paper for shopping lists, playing games with your family (a surprising number require making lists, drawing pictures, etc.), and so on.

be able to physically move chapters around, and you need to be able to make notes to yourself about changes you want to make.

Doing this level of revision on paper will make you more efficient because you won't be tempted to stop and actually make the planned changes. You'll want to go through the whole manuscript before you do that because, for example, a change you decide to make in chapter 5 might affect a change you thought you wanted to make in chapter 2.

In this revision, you're looking at the big picture; we'll start at the chapter level. Write your statement of argument at the top of a fresh sheet of paper and read your manuscript – note that at this point you are reading for the content, not editing the presentation. For each new chapter, write the chapter title and the statement of argument for that chapter.

When you finish your list, read your primary statement of argument and the statements for each of your chapters. Are they all on topic? Are they in a logical order? This is the time to think about chapter level organisation. Ask yourself whether it's clear why chapter 2 must come after chapter 1 and before chapter 3? To test whether this organisation is logical to others, try typing the statements of argument for each of your chapters and alphabetising them; then, email them to a trusted friend and ask her to number them in the order she thinks they go in. If her order is the same as yours, you've likely made the logic behind the progression clear. If it's not the same, talk to her about why she chose the order she did and determine whether you need to reorder your chapters, or you need to state your logic more explicitly.

When you're happy with the order of your chapters, it's time to move on to the paragraph level. For each chapter, write the statement of argument at the top of a new sheet of paper and read the chapter. As you read, write a one sentence summary of each paragraph - this is called reverse outlining, and you'll note that it is much more detailed than the kind of outline I suggest you start out with.

I recommend using a rough outline for the first draft, so you have the freedom to let the book develop; you need a more detailed outline now to help you shape the book to be useful for your readers.

As you create your reverse outline, if you come across any paragraphs that you can't summarise in a simple sentence, write two or more but also mark that paragraph for revisions. When you need multiple sentences to summarise one paragraph, it generally means that the paragraph isn't as focused as it needs to be.

You need to think about paragraphs as units of information; if you try to make one paragraph convey two or more significant points, you'll lose focus. More importantly, though, your reader will lose focus and either get frustrated with you or confused about what you're saying.

At the reverse outline stage, don't fix any unfocused paragraphs, just make a note or put a check mark next to it and move on.

You can either do this for all the chapters at once, or just one at a time. I tend to prefer to outline a chapter, ask myself the questions listed below for that chapter, and then repeat the process for the next chapter.

Whatever you decide, once you have an outline for a chapter, read through the outline and ask yourself the following questions:

- Do I make these points in a logical order?
- Do I stay focused on my statement of argument for this chapter?
- Do I cover everything I need to in order for my reader to understand what I'm explaining or teaching here?
- If I'm teaching a step by step process, have I included all the steps, or have I made assumptions about my reader's knowledge?

I want to spend some time looking at this last question. The most useful writing assignment I ever had in school was when I was about 15 and my English teacher asked us to write instructions for how to make a simple sandwich for someone who didn't know their way around our kitchen and who didn't know what a sandwich was - this was in the US, so the sandwich in question was peanut butter and jelly.

Of course, our first instinct was to write something along these lines: 'get the bread and spread peanut butter and jelly on it'. What our teacher was going for was more along these lines:

> First, open the cupboard to the left of the refrigerator and take out the loaf of bread and the jar of peanut butter; place these on the countertop. Then, open the refrigerator and take out the grape jelly (it's in the

centre of the top shelf). Next, open the cupboard above the dishwasher and take out a plate, and then open the drawer to the right of the dishwasher and take out two knives. Place all of these items on the countertop; now you're ready to make your sandwich.

A sandwich is made up of two slices of bread with a filling of some sort in the middle ...

You'll notice that these instructions don't assume the reader is completely unfamiliar with Western kitchens – I've assumed words like *cupboard* and *refrigerator* will be understood. However, since my teacher said the reader didn't know what a sandwich was or where things were kept in my kitchen, I've had to go into more detail than 'get the bread and other stuff you'll need to make your sandwich'.

As you write your book, you'll always be trying to strike a balance between treating your readers like the intelligent people they are and not frustrating them by assuming they have more specialist knowledge than they do. We'll talk more about beta readers in Chapter 17, but this is one of the reasons it is so important to choose at least one beta reader who is not a specialist in your topic.

PREPARING TO MOVE

Once you finish reading your paper draft, it's time to re-order your electronic text. This can get messy.

To ensure you don't accidentally delete anything, save a copy of your first draft. Name it something like 'draft 1 copy'.

Next, open a blank document and save it as 'draft 2'. Now you're ready to start moving text.

CUT AND PASTE[5]

Using your marked up hard copy as a guide, cut chunks of text from 'draft 1 copy' and paste them into 'draft 2'. I don't recommend trying to move more than a couple of pages at a time. If you do, you might accidentally move something to the wrong place.

To speed things up when, for example, you need to move a paragraph that was originally on page 50 to page 2, use the find function. In Word, simply type ctrl+f and type the first few words of the section you're looking for. Make sure you type them exactly as they were typed in the original; unlike many search engines, Word won't try to guess what you meant.

As you move through each page of your hard copy, be careful to keep it in order – you'll need it for the next step. Once you've re-ordered your entire draft to match the changes you made in your hard copy, save 'draft 2' and begin your second revision.

---

[5] If you don't know how to cut and past text, you'll find help on the internet. If you're using Microsoft Word, this video will help: http://bit.ly/2VUphya

Note: sometimes we decide upon reading draft 1, that some material needs to be cut entirely. It happens, but don't simply delete it. Keep this material in 'draft 1 copy' (it should be the only material left in that document after you finish cutting and pasting), so you'll have it should you ever want to return to it. Also, it can be easier to cut material that really needs to go, if it doesn't feel like you're just throwing it out. Writing takes work, and no one likes wasted effort.

CHAPTER 16
SECOND REVISION

NOW you get to start making sentence level changes!

First, read your hard copy again, but this time you're looking for sentence level issues. This is when you rework awkward sentences and consider things like tone and word choice. You may find it easier to work with your marked-up text if you use a different colour pen or pencil to make your changes than you used in the first revision.

This reading will likely take longer than the last one, but don't let perfectionism slow you down. You are trying to make your book better, not perfect.

WHAT TO LOOK FOR

As you read, you need to keep in mind what kinds of things you know you are able to fix and what things you'll leave to someone else. For example, if you've never really understood how to use commas, semi-colons, and colons correctly, you need to decide if it's something you want to learn, or something you want to pay an editor to fix for you.

TYPOS AND CONTINUITY ERRORS

As you read, you'll likely notice words that you frequently mistype. If your mistyped word is an actual word, spell check can't help you. Keep a list of your problem words on a separate sheet of paper, along with any words you know you tend to mix up (affect/effect, practice/practise, and so on). When you return to your electronic copy, use the find feature (ctrl+f) to search for the words on your list (and your usual mistyped versions of them). If one of your problem words is very short (say, you consistently type *to* when you mean *two*), you may get false-positives in the search results. To reduce these, type a space before and after the word you're searching for. That way, when you're searching for *to*, you won't also get all the instances of *towards, into*, or *toes*.

Also, make sure you are alert to any continuity issues. For example, if you discuss a hypothetical client in your book and she's called Martha in chapter 2 but Margaret in chapter 5, you need to pick a name. This may seem like a minor issue, but these things really annoy some readers - just as continuity errors annoy TV and film viewers. If you need proof of this, just google "continuity errors" and see how many videos come up.

PUNCTUATION

Punctuation causes a lot of confusion, and too often it seems that writers just throw their hands up and stop trying.

I am **not** criticising teachers here, but a lot of the anxiety writers feel around punctuation goes back to their experiences at school. Some of you will have had teachers who had to follow a curriculum that used a lot of jargon that English grammarians borrowed from Latin, while others will have had a curriculum that took a more relaxed approach (these are the 'use a comma where you would take a breath' teachers). Many of us will have had both sorts of teaching, and herein lies the problem.

I had a combination of approaches at school until I was about 14; from that point, if you were in the 'advanced' English classes you were expected to learn how to write from what you read. I understand the logic behind that, but no one ever learned how to properly form or punctuate a sentence in (then) twentieth-century English from reading *Romeo and Juliet* or *Tom Sawyer*.

I was lucky enough to have a professor who took the time to help me with my writing when I was an undergrad. I was then able to build on that by reading lots of grammar and punctation books. However, unless you're setting out to be an editor and/or writing coach, you don't need to read a stack of grammar books – you're probably relieved to hear that!

If you decide you want to take the time to learn how to use punctuation correctly, get a copy of *The Penguin Guide to Punctuation* by R. L. Trask. It's the most readable book on punctation that I've ever come across, and it's the one recommended by the Chartered Institute of Editing and Proofreading (https://www.ciep.uk/standards/) (if anyone knows this stuff, they do). One caveat, at the end when he discusses writing on the internet, it's amusingly clear that the book was written in 1997 and he didn't think this whole email thing was going to take off; either skip or quickly skim that bit.

If you really cannot face learning any punctuation rules, just do the best you can and then hire a copy editor.

CLICHÉS

Clichés are phrases that we've used so often that we've forgotten that they were once figures of speech. One is 'lighting fast'. We now take that to mean really fast. However, at one time it was recognised as a metaphor and related to the discovery that light travels faster than sound (that's why we see lighting before we hear thunder – unless the lightning is very close to us).

The occasional use of cliché is fine. It only becomes irritating for the reader when you use lots of clichés close together or, worse, misuse them.

ANECDOTES

Anecdotes, like clichés, are sometimes useful. However, if you have too many of them or they aren't clearly relevant to what you're saying, they are very irritating for your readers. If you've ever seen the movie *American Pie* (1999), you'll understand this. Alyson Hannigan's character Michelle annoys everyone else by always going on about 'this one time at band camp'.

A well-placed, well-chosen anecdote is a beautiful and powerful thing. However, if it feels like you're just throwing anecdotes at your reader to see what sticks, your reader will get annoyed and close the book.

FIGURATIVE LANGUAGE

Unless you are very unusual, you use figurative language every day. Think about the last time you tried to explain how something felt. Think about the first time you fell in love. Could you put it into language? Could you really explain how you felt without comparing your feelings to something else?

To give another example, doctors have us do this when we present with pain. If you go to the GP with a headache the doctor is likely to ask where the pain is located, followed quickly by questions like is it a stabbing pain? Or shooting? Or burning?

They do this not to annoy you with lots of questions, but because our language doesn't have a good way of talking about pain. They need to know what kind of pain it is, if they are to have any hope of helping you find relief. If this sort of thing interests you, I suggest you read Elaine Scarry's *The Body in Pain* (1985).

Scarry discusses practical uses of language in relation to pain, while literary scholars have written libraries full of books on figurative language over the years. For our purposes, you don't need to be an expert on figurative language; you just need to be aware of it when you use it in your writing.

You especially need to be aware when you misuse it.

MIXED METAPHORS

For those who need a refresher, a metaphor is a figure of speech in which you explain something by saying it is something else. Examples include 'she is crying rivers of tears' or 'she is a night owl'.

When you write, you need to check that you haven't mixed your metaphors. *The Independent* did a story on this in 2014.[6] I've quoted one of their examples here:

> 'They've put all their eggs in one basket and it's misfired' Paul Merson, Sky football pundit, of West Ham's purchase of Andy Carroll.

I don't really follow football but being an expert in football wouldn't help untangle these metaphors. We all know that when we 'put our eggs in one basket', we're depending too much on one thing working out; the comparison is to the inherent risk of putting all of your actual eggs in one basket – if you drop it, you'll have no eggs and a big mess. Misfire, however, refers to guns or similar weapons.

---

[6] You'll find the whole story here: https://www.independent.co.uk/arts-entertainment/books/features/the-top-ten-mixed-metaphors-9191302.html

Thus, the sentence would work if it read as follows: They've put all their eggs in one basket and dropped it. Instead, the sentence says that they put all their eggs in one basket and the basket has misfired. How can a basket misfire?

These are the kinds of logical questions you don't want your readers to waste their time pondering. When you do your final revision, check that you haven't inserted any equally baffling mixtures of metaphors.

CAUTION WITH SIMILES

Similes (comparing two things using like or as) are harder to abuse than metaphors, but it does happen. When you use a simile, make sure that either the connection between the two things is clear or make it clear in the context in which you use it.

We'll return to the example of telling your GP about your headache. If you told your GP that your headache felt like someone was pounding on the inside of your skull with a hammer, she'd have some idea what you meant. If, however, you told your GP your headache felt like a tree, you'd have some more explaining to do. I can't, right now, think of any obvious connections between headaches and trees, but I'm sure they're there somewhere.

Now that you've completed these checks, it's time to send your draft to your beta readers!

CHAPTER 17
BETA READERS

I discuss how to cope with any anxiety you have about letting others read your work in Chapters 19 and 20, 'Dealing with Criticism' and 'Dealing with Praise'. Here, I want to discuss how to choose your beta readers and help them help you.

CAN'T I JUST SEND IT TO MY PARTNER OR BFF?

This could work, but only if your partner or BFF is your ideal reader. I've written this book primarily for women business owners who want to write books about their businesses. Though my partner writes books, he is an academic, and that's a completely different kind of writing.

Of course, he can tell me whether the words on the page make sense, but he's not qualified to tell me if my book is what women business owners want or need to read.

When you choose beta readers, as far as possible, try to choose people who are your ideal readers. Social media can help here. Figure out where your ideal readers hang out, join them, support them, and ask for volunteers.

HELP THEM HELP YOU

The generous souls who volunteer as beta readers genuinely want to help you. However, if you just send them your manuscript and say, 'tell me what you think', they will likely be overwhelmed, and you may be disappointed.

To help both of you, send your beta readers some specific questions, like these:

- What do you think of my tone? Is it too formal or overly familiar?
- Which sections did you find confusing? Why?
- Which parts were too long?
- Which sections need more detail or development?
- Which parts did you particularly like? Why?
- Do you have any other feedback to help me make this book better?

Your list may not be identical to mine, but you should try to elicit both positive and negative feedback. Also, don't get too hung up on having answers to all of your questions. They should only be there as a guide.

WORD, GOOGLE DOC, PDF...?

Before you send your draft to your beta readers, you need to find out which format they're able to read or prefer. If they don't have a word processing program on their computer, you need to know that before you send them a Word document. If they use Google docs, but you use Word, it will be fine. Google docs can read Word files and vice versa. Whichever processor you use, make sure your beta readers turn on the function that tracks their changes[7] so you can see what they change in your document. They can also insert comments[8] if they need to ask for clarification or make some other comment. If one of your readers prefers to read a PDF, simply save a copy of your document as a PDF and send it to them. They can then use the Sticky Note[9] tool to comment on the text. If they don't have a PDF reader, they can download Adobe Acrobat for free.

DEADLINES

Make sure all deadlines are reasonable. Don't promise your beta readers the manuscript before you can reasonably complete it – you'll look unprofessional if you leave them waiting for it. Also, give them about a month to read it. That should be enough time for them to read it without throwing the rest of their schedule into chaos, but not so much time that they forget about it.

You'll need to time getting feedback from your beta readers around when you need to send your manuscript to your proofreader, so do keep that in mind when you are working

---

7   To learn to use Track Changes in Word, see this page: https://helpx.adobe.com/uk/acrobat/using/commenting-pdfs.html. For Google docs, see this page: https://support.google.com/docs/answer/6033474?co=GENIE.Platform%3DDesktop&hl=en
8   This function is in the 'review' menu for Word and the 'insert' menu for Google docs.
9   You'll find instructions for using the Sticky Note tool here: https://helpx.adobe.com/uk/acrobat/using/commenting-pdfs.html

out your schedule. Do not leave your proofreader waiting for your manuscript. She will have blocked time in her work schedule for you; if you don't deliver, she'll lose money, and you'll run the risk that she'll be too busy to help you when you do finally complete the manuscript.

One of the advantages of having 3 to 4 beta readers is that if one of them has an emergency and cannot meet your deadline, you'll still have enough feedback to carry on with finishing your book.

RESPONDING TO BETA READERS' FEEDBACK

When you send your manuscript to your beta readers, you need to remember that you're asking them for feedback so you can make your book better. A good beta reader will give you a balanced, well-considered response to your book.

Bad beta readers take two forms:

1) The kind who says it's awful and you must start again but doesn't give you any constructive criticism.
2) The kind who says it's brilliant and doesn't need any more work.

Both extremes are bad for you as a writer. The first because it's lazy, mean, and untrue. The second because it's lazy and untrue. These kinds of readers are using your book to exorcise other issues. The first is angry about something, and the second sees everything you do through rose tinted glasses. This is why your mum may not be a good beta reader for your book.

You may be thinking, but if the second says I'm brilliant, how can that be bad? It's bad because it doesn't help you make your book better. Every book can be improved; there is simply no such thing as a perfect piece of writing.

When you get feedback from your beta readers, if they're bad beta readers, take everything they say with a healthy pinch (or 3) of salt. If they're good beta readers, you need to be objective when you read their feedback.

A good beta reader will praise some sections and criticise others. You need to acknowledge both. Writers have a tendency to fixate on the criticism and not notice the praise.

Why is it important to notice the praise? Because you need to know what worked so you can do more of that in the future. You need to notice the criticism so you can fix whatever's wrong with your book.

Do you have to make all of the changes your beta readers suggest? Of course not. It's your book. What you must do, though, is read and think seriously about their suggestions. Don't just read a piece of criticism and flippantly say, 'I'm not doing that'. Think about it, and if you don't want to do it, make sure you can explain (at least to yourself) why you aren't going to do it – make sure you have a valid reason and that you're not reacting out of emotion.

As you work through your readers' comments and answers to your questions, keep a list of changes you actually want to make to your text. When you finish that, it's time for the third revision. Open 'draft 2' and save a copy as 'draft 3'. Go through your list, one item at a time, and make the changes to the draft. When you finish 'draft 3', it's time to send your draft to your proofreader.

CHAPTER 18

WHAT HAPPENS WHEN YOU WORK WITH AN EDITOR?

IN this chapter, when I write *editor*, I mean *all editorial professionals* (including developmental editors, copy editors, and proofreaders).

Sending your work to your editor can be stressful because you know she's going to read it more closely than anyone but you. This can make you feel overly exposed.

I can tell you that if you've hired a professional, she's seen it all before, but that isn't likely to do any more to calm your nerves than being told the doctor who's about to do an intimate examination of your body has 'seen it all before'.

These situations are stressful because we fear exposure and judgement. But our feelings are conflicted because we also want the professional in question to fix whatever's wrong, and they can't do that if they don't look.

WHY IS IT PARTICULARLY STRESSFUL TO SEND WORK TO AN EDITOR?

As I write this, I'm wondering why other situations in which we ask professionals to examine something don't bring up as much fear and anxiety as when we send our manuscripts to editors or take ourselves to the doctor (even just for a routine check-up). Think about the last time you took your car or your computer to the repair shop. Did you worry that the mechanic or technician was going to judge you? Did you feel exposed? Almost certainly not.

It's clear why a visit to the doctor is more anxiety provoking than one to the mechanic for an oil change. If the doctor finds something unexpected, it could have implications for your health and longevity. If the mechanic finds something, it may cost a bit more, but you are still going to be okay and live the rest of your life as expected.

Why does sending your work to an editor feel more like going to the doctor than taking your car to the mechanic?

A large part of why is that the writing comes from us. It feels like it is a part of us. It's really hard to see the editor fixing something in a draft in the same objective light in which we view a mechanic changing the oil in our car. Instead, it feels like the editor is finding fault with us, as people.

WHAT EDITORS DON'T DO

We don't pronounce judgement on you or your work. If your writing is riddled with punctuation errors, we won't judge you as a person or the quality of your book.

We also won't mark your work. We are editors, not teachers or lecturers. Your book is not an assessment, and our job isn't to judge your writing or your ideas.

WHAT EDITORS DO

We make suggestions to help you improve your writing. Most of us prefer to work in Microsoft Word so we can use Track Changes; that way, you can see what changes we think you should make. However, the final decision is yours. Our suggestions are focused on helping you make your book more accessible to your reader. It is always difficult for writers to look at their work from their reader's perspective - that's what your editor is there to do.

Good editors apply the 7 Cs - we make suggestions to make your text clear, concise, consistent, correct, coherent, complete, and credible.

WILL THE EDITOR EDIT OUT MY DISTINCTIVE WRITING VOICE?

No! Good editors work hard to maintain your voice, but we will tell you if your authorial voice feels inappropriate for the situation. For example, I edit both academic work and nonfiction books for general readers. These kinds of works require different authorial voices.

If one of my academic clients uses a lot of colloquialisms or contractions, I help her adopt a more formal tone. Equally, if I'm editing a nonfiction book that is meant to be a *popular* history of medicine that's chock full of scientific jargon that only a consultant would understand, I show the writer where the text has overestimated the ideal readers' abilities and suggest ways to make it more engaging and accessible.

WILL MY BOOK BE PERFECT WHEN I GET IT BACK FROM THE EDITOR?

Almost certainly not. Reputable editors never promise perfection. We're human. We know that we can and do make mistakes. What we do promise is that we make every effort to reduce the risk of making a mistake by using appropriate editorial tools and software and by keeping our skills up to date with continuing professional development courses.

For my own editorial work, I promise my clients that my work adheres to the high standards set by the Chartered Institute of Editing and Proofreading. I also promise to treat them and their text with respect.

CHAPTER 19

DEALING WITH CRITICISM

NO one likes being criticised, but you're writing a book and some reactions to your book may not be positive. You'll need to learn to deal with that reality.

I already talked about this a bit in Chapter 9, 'Writer's Block, Impostor Syndrome, and Other Things that Keep Writers up at Night'. Here, we're going to talk about all the criticism you'll have to deal with and where it will come from.

FEEDBACK FROM EDITORS AND PROOFREADERS

When you send your manuscript to an editor or proofreader, you are paying this person to give you feedback. Some will give you their reaction or summative response to the text in their email when they return the text to you; many will not.

Their job is to fix the text. These days, most will do this using the Track Changes feature in Microsoft Word. This lets you see what changes they think you should make and gives you the opportunity to accept or reject each of them.

For some reason, Word's default colour for Track Changes is red. When you couple this with the fact that Word marks every little change the editor makes on the page (when you have 'All Markup' selected in the dropdown menu under Tracking), the page can look like it's been splattered with blood.

If this bothers you, go into the advanced options for Track Changes and change the colour – you can have any colour you want: pink, turquoise, purple … Your editor cannot make this change for you – when you open the document on your machine, Word will go back to the default of red no matter what colour your editor used.

When you first open your document, resist the urge to assume it's all bad news or that all the changes mean that you're a terrible writer.

Instead, look at one change at a time. To make this easier, change the view to 200%, or more, so you can't see the whole page at once.

As you work through the changes, think about whether you want to accept or reject each one. This will take time. Though Word will let you just accept all, I don't recommend this.

You need to look at each change to learn from your editor (or proofreader) and also to make sure they've got it right. Editors will be the first to tell you they aren't always right. Sometimes they mess up because they've misread what you wrote, and other times because you haven't said what you meant to say.

Finally, as you work through the suggested changes, remember that your editor (or proofreader) is not judging you or your text. They're simply improving the words you sent them. Once you can see their interventions in your text as the helping hand it is, instead of as some sort of pronouncement of doom, you'll be a happier writer.

CRITICS, READERS, AND OTHER PEOPLE WITH OPINIONS

Once you publish your book and send it out into the world anyone who comes across it is free to pronounce their opinion on it.

Professional critics are not paid to be nice. If your book is reviewed by a professional, you get to choose whether to read that review or not. If you decide to read it, you need to remember that the critic is discussing your book, not you. No matter how brilliant or terrible they say it is, they're not talking about you as a person.

Before the internet, this chapter would have ended here. Thanks to the internet, the world seems to be full of amateur critics, from the people leaving reviews on Amazon to people posting on social media about the last book they read.

This makes avoiding reviews difficult. You need to develop a thick-ish skin, and you absolutely must know how to protect yourself.

If you attract the attention of a troll who keeps going on and on about your work, report them to the appropriate authorities and block them on all social media channels. For the less nasty critics out there, you're going to have to learn to ignore a lot.

On Amazon, read your 4- and 5-star reviews; the ego boost will help you with whatever writing project you undertake next. As for the lower ones, only pay attention to serious comments that can help you as a writer. Don't waste your time on the ones that are bordering on trolling behaviour. You just don't need to deal with people who hide behind the perceived anonymity of the internet to be rude to strangers.

If your readers contact you directly, read their emails (or direct messages). If they're being kind, or at least reasonable, respond. If they're trolls, block them from your account and move on with your life.

Above all, accept that you cannot please all the people all the time. Or, to paraphrase a meme I saw recently, if you were everyone's cup of tea, you'd be a mug.

FINAL WORD

This bears repeating: wherever criticism or perceived criticism is coming from, you need to remember that it has absolutely nothing to do with your worth as a person.

It has always been scary to do anything as public as publishing a book because publicity invites comment.

Thanks to the internet, that has been magnified at least 100-fold.

If you find that you can't stop yourself from looking at reviews, or you're fixating on negative feedback, please talk to someone.

CHAPTER 20

DEALING WITH PRAISE

INITIALLY, you might think dealing with praise is easy; you just smile, thank whoever's praising you, and move on. In the moment, this may well be the case.

What happens after? What happens when you start seeing people recommend your book because you're the expert on the subject?

Some of you will be chuffed to bits, and this kind of praise and attention will give you a little confidence boost. If you know this is how you will respond, you probably don't need to read this chapter.

For the rest of you, this kind of attention can raise all sorts of uncomfortable feelings.

I'M NOT REALLY AN EXPERT, AM I?

In Chapter 9, I suggested some ways you could deal with impostor syndrome when it rears its ugly head during the writing process. If you're not used to hearing other people refer to you as an expert, you're likely to experience impostor syndrome after you publish your book.

Logically, you will understand that their response is only to be expected. Our culture values authors and what they have to say. Once you become a published author, people will value what you have to say in the same way.

Remember, one of the main reasons you wrote your book was to establish your credibility and expertise in your field. Nevertheless, it may be jarring when you hear someone call you an expert.

You may find this disconcerting because it's new. If this is the case, start thinking of yourself as an expert now. Once you believe you are an expert, it won't surprise you to hear that others see you that way too.

If you resist this attention because it is attention and you're an introvert, you'll need to sit with those feelings. A lot of writers are introverts. I went to an event with the novelist Ben Aaronovitch when he was promoting his first novella *The Furthest Station* (2017), and in his explanation of why the evening was going to be a question and answer period rather than a talk, he said it was because he doesn't like giving talks. He recognised he was an introvert and said something to the effect of, 'I choose to spend my days behind my computer because I like it that way'.

Aaronovitch accepts that as a successful novelist, he has to get out and meet his fans because his publisher insists on it and it helps sales. He does not accept that he has to like doing it. The good news for you is that by self-publishing your book, you won't have any pressure from the publisher. Also, business books only require the writer to give talks and make public appearances when the writer chooses to. For example, Carrie Green (*She Means Business*), clearly works very hard at having a public persona. If that's not for you, don't do it.

Writers have long had trouble accepting praise, and I know that many of the great Victorian novelists avoided it as actively as they avoided criticism. For example, George Eliot (pen name for Marian Evans) avoided all reviews of her work. The negative ones would make her think of never writing again, and the positive ones made her fear she would never write so well again. It was only by avoiding reviews that she was able to keep writing and produce *Middlemarch* (1872), arguably the best realist novel in English. She did, however, learn to accept that fans would visit her to express their praise.

As you think about how to shape your public author persona, remember that if you've chosen to get your message out through writing a book instead of (rather than in addition to) creating a YouTube channel or some other medium that would put you in front of the camera, you may have made the decision because it was most comfortable for you as an introvert.

Introverts are often very sensitive to other people's feelings and reactions. Try not to let your fear of attention keep you from doing what you want to do. Your message matters and the world needs to hear (or read) it.

When positive attention to your book makes you uncomfortable, try to sit with the feeling. Explore both how you feel and why you feel the way you do. If you feel able, talk to a trusted friend about your response.

Also, trust that with time, though you may never revel in the attention, you will get used to it. Please, start thinking of yourself as an expert now, and however you feel, try very hard not to contradict someone who says you are an expert. That kind of contradiction is rude because it suggests the other person doesn't know what they're talking about.

FEAR OF BEING FOUND OUT

Sometimes discomfort with praise is just impostor syndrome, which can appear at this stage as the fear of being found out. If you hear someone talk about how good your book is, you may have to struggle with the fear that it's a fluke and you're not really as smart as they think you are.

Clearly, our brains can be real jerks sometimes.

If you have this kind of reaction, smile and be gracious to whomever you speaking to. Later, think about why you feel this way. Just sit with it until it makes some kind of sense. Then, remind yourself that *you* wrote your book. It was a long process that required a lot of intelligence and hard work.

It is not a fluke.

FEAR OF LETTING OTHERS (OR YOURSELF) DOWN

This one is closely related to the fear of being found out. As other people's praise lifts you up, you may start to worry that the only way to go is down. This is a form of catastrophising, or the belief that the worst possible outcome is the most likely (or only possible) one.

As with the other fears, sit with it until you understand it. Then, look at all the evidence you have to the contrary. You've succeeded at things in the past and gone on to have other successes. If this feeling comes up frequently, keep a list of all your past successes in your wallet to refer to as needed.

I've worked with one writer who was determined to hold onto their belief that the only way to go was down. They used the example of a one-hit-wonder music group. I countered by pointing out that the group didn't suddenly lose their ability to produce good music; what changed was how the record companies and radio stations (this was before services like Spotify were widely available) promoted them. If the people can't access their music, they can't buy enough copies to produce another hit.

You're luckier than the music groups who disappeared after one hit. Your expertise is yours. You don't depend on record labels or publishing houses for it. If you've ever responded to success by assuming it was an accident, start working now to really own your expertise.

I'M NOT ALLOWED TO BE AN EXPERT

If this kind of thought pops into your head, I have a question: 'Really, who said you couldn't be an expert?'

You may not have gone to a fancy public school and then on to Oxbridge, but you absolutely *are* allowed to be an expert.

Before you could write your book, you had to learn your field inside and out – that makes you an expert. You don't have to be *the* expert (if such a creature really exists), but you are *an* expert.

If you are reluctant to own your expertise because of teachers, parents, or employers criticising you over the years, work on believing that your opinion is the only one that matters. Or as the now clichéd meme says, other people's opinions are none of your business.

Also remember that their reasons for criticising you could have any number of sources that have nothing to do with you; these range from their own sense of inadequacy to their fear that you would rise above them. It's also possible that they were criticising you at a time before you had found your niche.

Now you have found what you're good at. Own your expertise.

CHAPTER 21
RESPECTING INTELLECTUAL PROPERTY

I expect my readers to have a variety of educational backgrounds, so I'll start at the beginning of what intellectual property (IP) is and why you need to make sure you respect other people's IP. If this is familiar ground for you, skim it to see if you learn anything new and move on to the next chapter.

We'll start with the UK government's definition:

> Intellectual property is something unique that you physically create. An idea alone is not intellectual property. For example, an idea for a book doesn't count, but the words you've written do. (https://www.gov.uk/intellectual-property-an-overview)

Failure to respect IP can lead to legal proceedings. Many of you will be aware of that so far as trademarks and patents are concerned, but it applies to all creative and written work, as well.

For this book, we're most concerned with written work. In the UK (if you live elsewhere, check the laws in your country), written work is automatically protected by copyright. You don't have to register it anywhere. If you want to make sure you remind your readers of this, simply include the copyright statement as I've done on page 2 for this book.

When you're doing research for your book, it's important to remember that copyright applies to all written work you consult, quote, or paraphrase. If you want to learn more about what's protected and when you might need to apply for protection, have a look at the gov.uk site I cited above (or your country's equivalent).

AVOIDING INTELLECTUAL PROPERTY INFRINGEMENT

Intellectual property infringement is called plagiarism. Another way of thinking about it is presenting someone else's work as your own. This is the definition that is most often used when introducing the topic to undergraduates.

At school, at least when I was at school, the word *plagiarism* wasn't usually used, but we were told not to copy from our peers' work or from books (I finished school in 1995, and I don't recall really being aware of the internet at that point).

GIVING CREDIT WHERE CREDIT'S DUE

So, what should you do if you need to reference someone else's work? You can adopt the system I've used in this book of citing the sources in the text. For the quotation from the gov.uk page on intellectual property that I used above, I mentioned the source (UK government) of the quotation before I gave the quotation and gave my readers the link to find the quotation themselves in parentheses after the quotation.

If the source had been a named author, it would look like this:

> <u>In *No Plot? No Problem!* Chris Baty encourages writers to stay hydrated; he says,</u> 'Beverage scientists have discovered that dehydration is one of the main factors in making a person feel tired' (82).

Here, the underlined words are mine and the words enclosed in inverted commas are Baty's. I've given the page number in parentheses.

When introducing the idea, I've used a shortened form of the full title: *No Plot? No Problem! A Low-Stress, High-Velocity Guide to Writing a Novel in 30 Days*. I've shortened this in the text because the reader doesn't need the full title to make sense of the point about staying hydrated. I'll give the full title in my works cited list (aka bibliography).

It's obvious that you need to cite direct quotations. What is less obvious is that you need to cite anything that you paraphrase or summarise.[10] The purpose of the citation is to give credit to your source. When in doubt, cite it. Your editor can help you remove any unnecessary citations.

Finally, remember that it is possible to plagiarise yourself. If all of your work is self-published, this isn't likely to cause any problems. However, if you publish something through a traditional publishing house or in a collection for which someone else owns the copyright, it could become an issue.

HELPING YOUR READER FIND YOUR SOURCES

At the end of your book, you'll need to include a works cited list. This, unsurprisingly, is a list of all the sources you cite as I've explained in the previous section.

Since your book isn't an academic work, you don't need to adopt one of the (sometimes) complicated citation systems used by academics. Instead, you need to find a format that is consistent and that gives the reader all the information they need.

In trade books (the kind you're writing), you'll often have these divided by source type. In other words, you'd have one list for websites and another for books and print articles. The works cited entries for the two sources I've used in this chapter would look like this:

---

[10] When you paraphrase a part of a text, you change the words and sentence structure but include all of the detail. When you summarise a text, your summary is in your own words and it only includes the main points.

Websites

Gov.uk. 'Intellectual Property and Your Work',
https://www.gov.uk/intellectual-property-an-overview

Books

Baty, Chris. *No Plot? No Problem! A Low-Stress, High-Velocity Guide to Writing a Novel in 30 Days* (Chronicle Books, 2014).

As you can see, these entries give the reader the information they need to find the source: author (or institution). Title (in inverted commas for short pieces, italicised for books), and publication information. Your editor will help you make sure these are formatted consistently, but it's your job as the writer to provide all the information.

GOOD PRACTICE FOR NOTETAKING

You need to start thinking about how you will manage your sources *before* you start to write. You *do not* want to go back through your draft trying to remember what needs to be cited and where it all came from.

To save you time and energy later, as you do your research, you need to get in the habit of clearly labelling each page of notes with the bibliographical information for the source. You also need to make sure any direct quotations you copy into your notes are enclosed in inverted commas and that they are followed with page numbers or website addresses.

Taking a moment to do this work when you're doing research will save you time later. It will reduce the risk of you accidentally plagiarising someone – this is rare, but it happens if your notes are sloppy.

Consider how this could happen. Let's say you ignore my advice and just jot down your own thoughts and a sentence you like from a book on the same piece of paper. Let's also assume you ignore my advice to always *enclose* direct quotations in inverted commas. Six months from now when you decide to include what you've written on that sheet of paper, are you going to remember which sentence was yours and which came from the book? Even if you do, will you know which book and what page?

GOOD PRACTICE FOR DRAFTING

As I've said before, when you're writing your first draft, you need to write as quickly as possible. To do this and save yourself a headache later, when you write something that needs a quotation and/or citation, come up with a system for signalling this. I use two asterisks (**) before each of these. Here's an example from the first draft of this chapter:

> If the source had been a named author, it would look like this:
>
> > In *No Plot? No Problem!* **?? Baty encourages writers to stay hydrated; he says, '**insert quotation here' (**).

> Here, the underlined words are mine and the words enclosed in inverted commas are Baty's. I've given the page number in parentheses.
>
> When introducing the idea, I've used a shortened form of the full title: *No Plot?* ***give full title here.* I've shortened this in the text because the reader doesn't need the full title to make sense of the point about staying hydrated. I'll give the full title in my works cited list (aka bibliography).

As you can see, I've included the information I could remember and used ** to tell myself what I need to find. Whatever signal you decide to leave yourself, make sure you always use the same one. When it's time for me to go back through my draft and fill in the stuff I left myself notes about, I can simply use the search function in Word (ctrl+F) to find all of the instances of ** in the text. When I finish, I'll run another search just to make sure I've removed all of them. This way, there's no danger of the book going to print with my notes in it. There's also no danger I'll forget to cite a quotation.

USE TECHNOLOGY IF NECESSARY

In 2020, it should come as no surprise to you that we have technology that can help us with these things. If you're writing a book that uses a lot of sources, you may want to take the time to learn how to use a citations manager like Zotero or End Note.

Don't download Zotero (it's free) or buy a citation manager just for the sake of having it. If you're not likely to have multiple citations on each page of your book, you probably don't need to spend your time learning how to use a citations manager.

CHAPTER 22
PRACTISE SAFE WRITING

IMAGINE having written 20,000 words of your book, saving it on your laptop, and having your laptop stolen. Alternatively, imagine finishing your first draft, saving it, and coming back to it the next day to find that your computer won't turn on at all.

I know writers who have had such experiences. To keep you from having to add your name to the list of the unfortunate, I want you to put some healthy habits in place before you start writing. In this chapter I'll address how to keep both hard copies and digital copies safe.

PROTECTING PAPER COPIES

Many writers still write their drafts out longhand before they type them up. I understand that for some people this both frees and focuses the mind. If you are one of these people, carry on, but take some precautions.

RISKS TO PAPER

FIRE
Massively destructive fires are, thankfully, less common than they used to be. But they aren't unheard of. For a few pounds, you can get a small fire safe in which to keep your completed manuscript pages/notebooks.

FLOOD
Don't store your manuscript on the ground floor, if your house is prone to flooding. Also, don't store it in the bathroom or kitchen.

Water and paper are not good friends. Water and ink get on less well. Try to choose a pen that doesn't run when it gets wet.

WILD ANIMALS
Okay, maybe not wild animals, but pets can wreak havoc with your paper manuscript. When she was younger, my cat took great pleasure in sliding my papers around the flat. Now, she takes pleasure in chewing on them. Keep an eye on your pets and keep your papers out of reach.

CHILDREN
If you have children, until they are old enough to understand that they mustn't touch your papers, keep them well out of reach. You don't want to come home to find that chapter 1 has been used for your little one's latest masterpiece, or to find that they've smeared the carrot they weren't happy about at lunch all over the first page.

BACKING UP YOUR WORK

Backing up a hardcopy requires work on your part. I recommend you do all of these:

- Get in the habit of photocopying or scanning new pages as you produce them.
- If you choose to scan them, skip to the next section: 'Protecting Digital Copies'.
- If you choose to photocopy your manuscript, keep a copy in your firesafe.
- In addition to this, at least once a month, take a second copy to store somewhere else – at a trusted friend's house, in your office (assuming you don't work at home), or in a safe deposit box at the bank.

You may think these suggestions are extreme, especially the safe deposit box, but think about how you'd feel if you lost your whole book before you could type it up and publish it. That would mean throwing dozens, if not hundreds, of hours away because you didn't take the time to back up your work.

PROTECTING DIGITAL COPIES

We'll start with how to keep it safe while you're actually writing and work forwards from there. We all know that the main risks to a digital copy are failure to save, virus infection, and power surges. Install good virus protection software and use a surge protector. For everything else, read on.

AUTOSAVE IS YOUR FRIEND

Word has an autosave function. If you're typing your manuscript in Word, click on File › Options › Save and then choose 1 minute for how often you want autosave to save your document. If you use another kind of software, it is worth your while to check whether it has a similar function.

HARD SAVE REGULARLY

If you haven't already, you'll soon learn that I don't trust computers. In addition to using autosave, get in the habit of manually saving your document at least once an hour. Doing this will massively increase your chance of saving everything should there be a power surge or should your computer take a funny turn.

SAVE TO A FLASH DRIVE AND/OR EMAIL YOURSELF A COPY

At least once a week, save a copy of your manuscript to a flash drive and/or email it to yourself. I suggest doing both just to be absolutely certain you don't lose anything. If you don't email it to yourself, make sure you keep your flash drive in a different building than the one you keep your computer in. You could also consider saving a copy in Google Docs - since that is not saved on your computer, so long as you don't get locked out of your Google account, you'll be able to access it.

INVEST IN THE CLOUD

Saving everything to the cloud is affordable and easy. If you didn't buy the cloud backup package when you bought your computer, now is the time to look into it.

PRINT A COPY

At the end of each draft, I strongly recommend that you print a copy and ask a trusted friend to keep it or store it in your office, if your office is not in your home. As I said above, I don't trust computers. Printing a copy, in addition to the other steps, guarantees that you will have a copy somewhere. Though computers sometimes seem to have minds of their own, paper always behaves as you expect it to.

If you've finished reading this and you think I'm just being alarmist, ignore this advice at your own risk. Losing your book draft is much worse than losing your homework or even a term paper could possibly be.

CHAPTER 23
STAYING ORGANISED

WHETHER you write longhand or on computer when you're writing your draft, you'll likely use both forms for taking notes. Organising your notes from the beginning will make your life easier later. If you don't naturally keep everything tidy and logically organised (goodness knows I don't), you're going to have to make the effort here. If you don't, you'll lose days of writing time to looking for a note you're sure to took and now need but can't find.

CORRAL YOUR PAPER

If at all possible, designate a certain notebook, or set of notebooks, to keeping your notes for your book to the exclusion of absolutely everything else. As I said in Chapter 21 when I was discussing how to use sources responsibly, make sure all quotations are enclosed in inverted commas and that the top of each page is clearly labelled, so you know what you're looking at months later when you return to that note.

Because of the nature of notebooks, you may find that you take notes on different topics in succession. When you have your rough outline, as you reread your notes, you can assign each chapter a colour and use coloured sticky tabs to show you where to look for particular topics. If your tabs are wide enough, you can write a reminder word or phrase on them to make things even easier.

If you have printed copies of articles or other loose bits of paper, you will need a useable filing system. The shape this system takes will depend on how much material you need to corral. During my PhD, I had a 4-drawer filing cabinet full of articles I'd marked up, but for this book I only need an accordion file.

Whichever system you choose, label each folder clearly. For some projects it will make sense to use the authors' names for the labels, for others it will be better to have a folder (or a few folders) devoted to each topic you're researching.

KEEPING DIGITAL FILES ORGANISED

This, in part, will involve developing a systematic way of using the files on your desktop to organise your documents. I'd suggest you use these levels

1) A folder for the whole project (this will make backing things up easier – you've only got the one big folder to transfer to your flashdrive).
    A) Within this folder, keep one for your drafts and one for your notes

I) Within your drafts folder, keep separate folders for different stages of the process.
II) Within your notes folder, consider organising your notes into topic folders.

KEEPING INDIVIDUAL FOLDERS ORGANISED

You need a system for naming individual documents that will mean something to you a month, or longer, after you save them.

For notes, you need to make sure the file name makes it easy for you to find it later.

For drafts, you'll need to name both the draft number and the date. For example:

D1 21-04-19

This means draft 1 was saved on the 21st of April 2019. For your first draft, the date may be unnecessary. For your second and subsequent drafts, you'll likely find it useful. These drafts will be sent to others for comment, and you'll be working on them while others do as well.

So, if I sent D1 21-04-19 to my editor, I'd rename the file with a new date the next time I worked on it. When I got it back from my editor, I'd change the name of the copy with her mark-up on it to something like D3 Smith 30-06-19. If my editor's surname were Smith, I'd know that this is the copy she's seen, and I'd have a record of the date on which

I saved the copy she sent me. Do the same for anyone else who gives you feedback.

If you're disciplined enough to do this consistently, you should always be able to find an earlier version when you need to.

BOOKS

If you have several books that are key to what you're writing about, find a shelf near your workspace on which to keep them. To make your life easier, also put the books in some sort of order.

I tend to prefer alphabetizing mine by the author's last name, but if that doesn't work for you, organise them by topic or something else that works for your purposes.

As with the other organisational tips, the point of this is to make it easier to find what you need when you need it.

CHAPTER 24

RECOMMENDED READING

I'VE organised this list by type of book to make it easier for you to find what you're looking for. The little write up below each entry explains why I find the book useful and should help you decide whether it's the kind of thing you want to read yourself.

Whatever you do, don't let this list keep you from writing. You can write your first draft without reading any of these. However, if you run into problems, one or more of them may prove useful.

GRAMMAR, PUNCTUATION, AND USAGE

Trask, R. L. *The Penguin Guide to Punctuation* (Penguin Reference, 1997).

> This little book is actually readable, which is surprising given its topic. For those of you who don't find the topic of punctuation as interesting as I do, it's also very easy to dip in and out of. Each type of punctuation gets its own chapter, and each chapter

ends with a summary of the points it covered. The best thing about this book, though, is that it doesn't use a lot of specialist jargon. If you are reasonably good at reading in English, you'll be able to understand this book. This is the kind of book you need on hand for all of your business writing (emails, web copy, blog posts, articles, books, ...); it's inexpensive and available in paperback.

New Hart's Rules: The Oxford Style Guide, 2nd ed.
(Oxford University Press, 2014). (For UK English)

This book isn't designed to be read cover to cover. Instead, it really is the kind of reference book in which you look up what you need to know and leave the rest. It does use some specialist language, but don't let that put you off. If you live in the UK, you'll likely find a copy of this (though possibly not the most recent edition) in your local library. It's not a book you're going to need to consult often enough to justify buying a copy unless you plan to write one or more books a year from here on out or become an editor.

Chicago Manual of Style, 17th ed.
(University of Chicago Press, 2017). (US English)

Like *New Hart's Rules*, this is a reference book; if you ever see a hard copy of this 1145-page manual, you'll be glad I didn't suggest you need to read the whole thing. You'll only need to consult this book if you decide to write in US English. If your business is based in the UK and most of your customers are based here too, you don't need to worry about this one.

DICTIONARIES

UK ENGLISH

New Oxford Dictionary for Writers and Editors (Oxford University Press, 2005).

> This dictionary is invaluable for spelling (surprise!) and determining use of italics, hyphens, and diacritical marks (accents). For example, it tells us that the word *nécessaire* (a case for small items) needs to be italicised and keeps the accent over the *e*. Keeping the accent and italicising the word means that it hasn't been used in English long enough for it to be fully anglicised. Meanwhile, it says naive can be spelled naïve (with the accent over the *i*), but it isn't italicised.
>
> You may be thinking, 'but people don't care about this sort of thing'. I'd say they don't, to a point. If a writer switched back and forth between naïve and naive, it would irritate a great many of your readers. It's also useful to have chosen a standard dictionary so your editor/proofreader will know which one to consult if they have any queries.
>
> This dictionary is not great for definitions. If you just need a quick reminder of what a word means, it will do. If it's a new word for you, or you want examples of how to use it, you'll likely want a more detailed definition.

For less specialist uses, you'll find perfectly serviceable dictionaries online.

> You'll get more reliable information from sites like Oxford Dictionaries (https://en.oxforddictionaries.com/) and Cambridge Dictionaries (https://dictionary.cambridge.org/), than from some of the others Google will give you. This isn't a case of intellectual snobbery; it's a case of not always trusting what I find on the internet.
>
> Dictionaries compiled by well-known academic publishers are compiled and maintained by properly trained professionals. When they give you an example of how to use a word, they've checked that it's correct. Some other dictionaries are crowdsourced. Crowdsourcing is great for many, many things, but compiling a reliably accurate dictionary is not one of them.

For etymology and word history, you'll need to consult the Oxford English Dictionary (OED): https://www.oed.com/.

> This is not to be confused with the Oxford Dictionaries site I discuss above. The OED is a massive dictionary that is continuously updated. Work on it began in 1857 and continues today. For most users, the OED gives way too much information. However, if you need to understand the history of a word, it can't be beat. If you live in the UK, your local library can probably help you access it. If you are or know a university student or staff member, you can probably access it that way.

US ENGLISH

> For US English, *Merriam-Webster* is my preferred dictionary; Americans tend to call it *Webster's* for short. You can access it here: https://www.merriam-webster.com/. *Webster's* has been around since 1828; it is comprehensive and reliable.

BOOKS ABOUT HOW TO BE A WRITER

Baty, Chris. *No Plot? No Problem! A Low-Stress, High-Velocity Guide to Writing a Novel in 30 Days* (Chronicle Books, 2014).

> This does what it says on the cover. Since you're writing a non-fiction book about your business, you may be wondering why I'm recommending a book about how to write a novel. It's because this book is useful and succinct. You can, obviously, skim or skip the stuff on characterisation and setting, but the chapters on the life of a writer (finding time, overcoming self-doubt, etc.) are brilliant. Also, should you ever decide you want to participate in National Novel Writing Month (November, every year), you'll be ready.

Silva, Paul J. *How to Write a Lot: A Practical Guide to Productive Academic Writing*, 2nd ed. (APA LifeTools, 2018).

> I know this is a book written for academics, but it has a lot of really good advice on writing a lot

and writing quickly, even if you're busy. I know the media often portray academics as having lots of free time to think and write, but this is a myth. All of the academics I know could easily fill 40+ productive hours a week doing things for their jobs (teaching, meetings, supervising students, going to conferences, liaising with local councils and other groups, etc.) before they even start work on the research and writing they must do if they want to keep their jobs. Successful academics have to master the art of fitting writing in around a lot of other things, and this book shows them how to do it.

Jensen, Jolie. *Write No Matter What: Advice for Academics* (University of Chicago Press, 2017).

I know, I know, another book for academics. Stick with me on this one. Jensen's advice is brilliant. She's been teaching people how to write (and how to write more productively) for years. When I read her book, it was like having my undergraduate mentor (from the late 90s) speaking to me again. The advice she gives has been around for a long time. Writing teachers and coaches keep giving this advice because it works; Jensen has packaged it up in one little book.

WORKS CITED

PRINT SOURCES

Aaronovitch, Ben. *The Furthest Station* (Victor Gollancz Ltd., 2017).

Bradley, Lauryn, *Grow Your Tribe – How to Scale + Skyrocket Your Business by Loving Your Audience* (The Spectacular Media Group Ltd., 2019).

Baty, Chris. *No Plot? No Problem! A Low-Stress, High-Velocity Guide to Writing a Novel in 30 Days* (Chronicle Books, 2014).

Chicago Manual of Style, 17th ed. (University of Chicago Press, 2017).

Eliot, George. *Middlemarch*, edited by Rosemary Ashton (Penguin Classics, 1994; originally published 1872).

Green, Carrie. *She Means Business: Turn Your Ideas into Reality and Become a Wildly Successful Entrepreneur* (Hay House UK Ltd, 2017).

Jensen, Jolie. *Write No Matter What: Advice for Academics* (University of Chicago Press, 2017).

Lamott, Anne. *Bird by Bird: Some Instructions on Writing and Life* (Anchor Books, 1995).

New Hart's Rules: The Oxford Style Guide, 2nd ed. (Oxford University Press, 2014).

New Oxford Dictionary for Writers and Editors (Oxford University Press, 2005).

Scarry, Elaine. *The Body in Pain: The Making and Unmaking of the World* (Oxford: Oxford University Press, 1985).

Silva, Paul J. *How to Write a Lot: A Practical Guide to Productive Academic Writing*, 2nd ed. (APA LifeTools, 2018).

Sternberg, David. *How to Complete and Survive a Doctoral Dissertation* (St Martin's Press, 1981).

Trask, R. L. The *Penguin Guide to Punctuation* (Penguin Reference, 1997).

Wordsworth, William. *Preface to Lyrical Ballads*, in *Wordsworth & Coleridge, Lyrical Ballads*, edited by R. L. Brett and A. R. Jones, 2nd ed. (Routledge, 1991; originally published 1800).

ELECTRONIC SOURCES

Cambridge Dictionaries: https://dictionary.cambridge.org/

Godin, Seth. 'Talker's Block'. 23 September 2011. Retrieved from: https://seths.blog/2011/09/talkers-block/

Gov.uk. 'Intellectual Property and Your Work', https://www.gov.uk/intellectual-property-an-overview

Merriam-Webster Dictionary: https://www.merriam-webster.com/

Nowell, David D. 'Manage Procrastination with the Pomodoro Technique'. *Psychology Today*, 2 July 2013. Retrieved from: https://www.psychologytoday.com/gb/blog/intrinsic-motivation-and-magical-unicorns/201307/manage-procrastination-the-pomodoro-technique

Oxford Dictionaries: https://en.oxforddictionaries.com/

Oxford English Dictionary: https://www.oed.com/

Rentoul, John. 'The Top Ten Mixed Metaphors'. *The Independent*, 16 March 2014. Retrieved from: https://www.independent.co.uk/arts-entertainment/books/features/the-top-ten-mixed-metaphors-9191302.html.

Solomon, Solomon. 'The Surprising Solution to Imposter Syndrome'. TEDxCharlotte, 30 November 2016. Retrieved from: https://youtu.be/whyUPLJZljE

Verrusio, W., Ettorre, E., Vicenzini, E., Vanacore, N., Cacciafesta, M., and Mecarelli, O. 'The Mozart Effect: A Quantitative EEG Study'. *Consciousness and Cognition*, September 2015, vol. 35, pp. 150-5. Retrieved from: https://www.ncbi.nlm.nih.gov/pubmed/26036835

AFTERWORD

By Sam Pearce, SWATT Books (www.swatt-books.co.uk)

IF you've made it this far, it's safe to say that you have finished - or are well on your way to being finished - writing your first book. Great! But do you know how to get it into the hands of your readers?

Many great books never fully see the light of day or get lost in obscurity simply because their authors were not 100% familiar with the various processes involved in getting a book published properly and did not know how to best take advantage of all the tools and resources that are available in today's modern world of accessible publishing.

Jennifer has kindly asked me to give you a quick and simple run-down of the key steps that you need to follow to give your book the best chance of success. You will note that marketing is NOT a step listed here. That is because great book marketing is not a single step in itself, it is a process that you should be thinking about and implementing throughout the entire life cycle of your book - from the day you start writing it, through to its 1st anniversary and beyond.

If you do need some support with book marketing, a good place to start is *Book Marketing Made Simple* by Karen Williams (https://www.amazon.co.uk/Book-Marketing-Made-Simple-Practical/dp/0995739021), which looks at various marketing strategies that you can implement whilst writing your book; Williams also discusses how to launch it and how to keep the momentum going with book sales. You can also check out the Self-Publishing Advice Centre run by the Alliance of Independent Authors (https://selfpublishingadvice.org/category/book-marketing-for-indie-authors/), which has numerous blogs and resources dealing with book promotion and marketing across all genres.

The very first step in publishing a book is to WRITE it in the first place. I'm going to assume that as you've read this far into this book you have already done that or are well on your way. So we will pick up the process from where Jennifer leaves off.

Are you ready? Let's get to it!

BOOK DESIGN

As Jennifer mentioned in Chapter 5, book design is an instance where you want to invest in a professional. We've all heard the adage "Don't judge a book by its cover", but unfortunately that is exactly what most people do with books from an author that they have not heard of before.

I recommend that you engage a book designer at the same time as you send your manuscript for editing, as it saves time in the long run. While your editor is finessing your manuscript, your designer can be designing the cover and working out the template for the contents so that when the manuscript is out of editing, they can move straight into final typesetting.

This is also the stage where, with advice from your designer, you decide on what format your book will take and work out what your print specifications will be. Will it be paperback or hardback, what size will it be, do you need full-colour printing inside or will just black do? All of these decisions have an impact on your final book, and in particular, on its cover price and whether it is right for your market, so take your time with this step and heed the advice of your designer.

REGISTER WITH AN ISBN AGENCY

Once your designer has finished typesetting your book and you're in the artwork review stage, it is time to register with an ISBN agency and purchase a set of ISBNs. Any print book that you want to sell through traditional retail channels (such as Amazon) MUST have an ISBN. Though eBooks do not require an ISBN, it is in your best interest to apply one anyway, as it gives your book wider visibility within the book trade.

Be aware that many online publishing platforms, including Amazon's KDP, give you the option of using one of their ISBNs. Don't do it; always purchase your ISBNs and register them against your publishing imprint. Though the assignment of an ISBN is not an indication of copyright ownership, it does give the owner of the ISBN certain rights over the management of your book. By purchasing your own ISBN's it ensures that you retain 100% of the rights to your book. It is also worth noting that ISBNs are non-transferable, and they do not expire. So, any ISBNs you purchase will always be available to you no matter how long it is before you decide to write your next book (or update your first one with a second edition).

Here is a list of the main ISBN agencies for major territories:

United Kingdom & Ireland: Nielsen Book
www.isbn.nielsenbookdata.co.uk

United States: R.R. Bowker, LLC
www.isbn.org

Canada: Canadian ISBN Agency, Library and Archives Canada
www.bac-lac.gc.ca/eng/services/isbn-canada

France: AFNIL
www.afnil.org

Australia: Thorpe Bowker
www.myidentifiers.com.au

Spain: Agencia del ISBN
http://agenciaisbn.es

After you have received your ISBNs, you need to forward the ones that you are using for this book to your designer, so they can add them to your copyright page (this is a legal requirement) and generate a scannable barcode to be applied to the back cover artwork.

EBOOK CONVERSION

Not all books are suitable for the eBook format (such as image-intensive art books), but you should always consider having an eBook edition of your book available, as it increases your potential sales. Some readers will only purchase a printed edition of a book; however, there is an increasing number of readers who prefer to purchase eBooks (usually for convenience or environmental reasons). Let's not forget the die-hard book worms who will buy a print edition for their libraries AND an eBook edition for convenience when commuting or going on holiday, which allows you to sell your book twice to the same reader.

A good book designer should be able to do the conversion for you as well as perform all the necessary testing to make sure the eBook works on various types of eReaders such as Kindle, Nook, Kobo, and iBooks, as well as smartphones and tablets. If they can't do the conversion as part of the design process, then you will need to hire an eBook specialist who is familiar with the background coding that is required to make eBooks work efficiently.

SETTING UP YOUR PUBLISHING ACCOUNTS

Registering for self-publishing accounts with IngramSpark and KDP (Kindle Direct Publishing) is free of charge,[11] and when used in conjunction, they are by far the most robust self-publishing method out there right now. I advocate the use of a dual publishing model because with KDP your book gets priority listing across Amazon, whilst IngramSpark gives your book access to a wider international distribution network (such as Waterstones, Barnes & Noble, Chapters/Indigo, and over 7,000 other book retailers).

Both IngramSpark and KDP use a Print on Demand (PoD) production model. This means that you don't need to invest in printing hundreds of books upfront; copies of your book are printed as and when they are ordered. This makes the process of publishing your first book less of a risk, and it is much cheaper and far simpler than paying a printer to print a bulk order of books and then managing the storage and distribution of those books yourself – all in the hopes that you will be able to sell them.

You can find more information about IngramSpark on their website at www.ingramspark.com, and more about KDP at https://kdp.amazon.com.

---

[11] Note that there is a one-off listing fee for each title published on IngramSpark. At the time of publication that fee was $49USD for publishing a print and eBook edition of the same title at the same time. See www.ingramspark.com/pricing for more details.

LISTING YOUR BOOK

Now we get to the publishing part of your journey - listing your book. There are several things you need to think about beforehand to optimise your book sales, such as title, description, author details, keywords, genre & categories, metadata, reviews, cover price, market availability, wholesale discount, return-ability, and on-sale date.

I recommend doing your homework before starting the listing process. See what other authors of similar books have included in their listings, what categories they have listed in, and what cover price they are asking. Then put yourself squarely into your readers' shoes and think about what will make them buy your book instead of any of the others.

Getting the listing details for your book right is vital to your book being both found and ultimately purchased, so really take your time with this step. Also, don't be afraid to do some trial and error testing. One of the major benefits of self-publishing is that you can update your listing information at anytime once your book has been published. If your sales aren't great, tweak your listing and then monitor for improvement.

ARTWORK SUBMISSION

Once you've got your title details listed, you need to upload all the artwork required for your book. This includes cover art and the interior for your book in both print and eBook formats (if required). Your artwork will go through a 2 step quality control process to ensure that it falls within production guidelines. On KDP this process is done in real-time, whereas on IngramSpark the process takes up to 3 business days to complete.

Note that if you are publishing an eBook, IngramSpark will automatically submit your eBook listing to retailers as soon as the artwork passes quality control. For this reason, I recommend setting your on-sale date for 2-3 weeks in the future if you are publishing both an eBook and a print edition. This ensures that you have enough time to complete the additional steps needed for the print book and both editions go on sale at the same time. If you do this, the eBook will still be listed straight away but set as pre-order only until the official on-sale date.

TEST PRINT

If you are publishing a print book, once the artwork passes inspection it is highly recommended to order a single test print copy of the book from both IngramSpark and KDP before releasing it for distribution. This will allow you to see exactly what your readers will receive and be the last opportunity you get to make any last-minute changes before the book goes on sale.

DISTRIBUTION & POD ORDER

Once you are happy with the quality and artwork of the test print copy of your book, it's time to give IngramSpark and KDP approval to release your book for public distribution. This releases the print edition of your book to be listed for retail sale alongside your eBook listing. Again, if you have set an on-sale date for the future, the listing will be set to pre-order until the official on-sale date.

Now is also the time for you to order a batch of print on demand (PoD) copies for your own sales fulfilment (such as through your website or in-person) and for marketing purposes. I recommend using IngramSpark for ordering your PoD copies as their ordering process is a bit easier to use (especially for shipping books to an address that is not your own) and their printing costs are generally a bit cheaper than KDP (though it's always worth comparing costs first).

BOOK DATABASE SUBMISSION

Though not a requirement, I highly recommend that you add the metadata for your book to the International Book Database which is accessible through the ISBN agency in your territory. These databases are used by thousands of bookstores and online retailers to monitor new book releases and gather information on titles they wish to stock in-store, so it's in your interest to provide the database with as much information as you can.

LEGAL DEPOSIT

The last step in the process is to provide your legal deposit copies. This is a legal requirement for print books in the UK, and many other major publishing territories. It simply requires you to send a copy of your printed book to a designated central library for public record.

If legal deposits are a requirement in your territory, your ISBN agency will notify you of the requirement when you purchase your ISBNs and provide you details on how to comply.

So that's the self-publishing process in a nutshell.

I understand that there is a lot of information here, and this covered several steps that you were probably not aware of.

If you are feeling a bit overwhelmed by what is involved in self-publishing, or just don't have the time to commit to the learning curve necessary to do your book justice, there are self-publishing agencies and consultants like me who can help you through the process. Just be sure to do your research and make sure that any agency or consultant you use will work on YOUR behalf and not publish your book using their accounts or ISBNs. Otherwise, it's not self-publishing; rather, it's a nasty form of hybrid publishing and you run the risk of not only losing control of your book but also losing a percentage of your royalties.

Printed in Great Britain
by Amazon